THIN WITHIN

THIN

Foreword

For twenty-five years in my medical practice I have tried to help people deal with eating and weight-related problems. Unfortunately 95 percent of those who want or need to lose weight never reach or maintain their ideal weight. This means we have about one chance in twenty of being successful using the traditional approaches to weight control.

We pay a tremendous price, both medically and psychologically, for being overweight. Obesity adversely affects every system in the body, including cardiovascular, respiratory, digestive, musculoskeletal, and endocrine. The emotional suffering of overweight people is impossible to imagine. Think of one lonely, depressed, tired, unfulfilled overweight person you know and multiply that misery by forty million, the number of Americans said to be seriously overweight.

I first learned of Thin Within in 1983 when I met Judy Wardell. I attended the workshops, found out how superb the program was and have been sending friends and patients to Judy and her staff ever since. Their results are so superior that I've discarded every other approach to weight-related problems.

Writing this foreword is a joy for me; Judy and I were married last year. This marvelous book contains everything needed to resolve problems with weight or eating disorders. *Anyone* who wants to can easily master his or her weight problem with the Thin Within method. Its direct and practical approach will amaze and delight you. Amaze because of what you will learn about yourself, and delight because you will permanently resolve your eating or weight problems *and* wonderfully change your life at the same time.

The Thin Within philosophy is a stroke of genius. By all means avail yourself of it. Your body will be eternally grateful.

Arthur W. Halliday, M.D.
University of California
School of Medicine
San Francisco, California

Introduction

What if I were to tell you that in 30 days I could give you all the tools you need to be thin without ever dieting again? What if I were to tell you that a phenomenal change will take place within you so that you will become *naturally* thin while eating anything you want and not depriving yourself? And what if I said this 30-day process will be so effective and enjoyable that you will literally melt down to your natural size and love doing it. This is exactly what Thin Within will do for you.

How can I make such an incredible claim? Because for the past twenty-three years I have been professionally involved with people and eating disorders. For the past ten years I have helped over twenty thousand people change their lives and lose weight in the most enjoyable way possible, eating *anything* they want, using the same thirty-five easy and practical Thin Within tools contained in this book. And I know personally, because after years of struggle I released 38 pounds and have kept it off effortlessly for ten years.

I was trained as a psychiatric nurse and did family, group, and individual counseling for years. I have long known that eating disorders involve much more than merely losing weight. I know because I've been on both sides of the fence—I've been naturally thin and I've been so overweight that I was embarrassed to be seen in public. I tried every possible diet, exercised myself silly (rehearsing six hours a day in a professional dance company), was bulimic for a year, and even had my jaws wired shut! And I always gained back the weight I lost. My experiences convinced me that permanent weight loss had to involve more than calorie counting. My instincts told me that diets didn't work.

After ten years' experience in Thin Within, I now know why. But first, let me state emphatically that Thin Within is not a diet. In Thin Within there's no weighing in, food plans, or calorie counting. It has nothing to do with will power, excruciating exercise, or group coercion. It is an easy, practical approach that has everything to do with losing all the weight you want, at the rate you want to, eating anything you want (from sweet butter to hot fudge sundaes), and keeping it off forever. In Thin Within we produce permanent, not temporary, results. It has been conclusively shown that the success rate of diets is between 2 to 5 percent, while an independent study of Thin Within demonstrated a long-term success rate of over 60 percent. Thin Within's graduates not only lose weight, they sustain that weight loss over time.

I came upon Thin Within while struggling with my own weight. I kept looking for a program that would embrace my entire being—body, mind, and spirit—an approach that would involve me physiologically *and* psychologically.

At this time I met Joy Imboden Overstreet, who had already put together the basic concept of Thin Within. We both had realized that we could lose weight and yet still be obsessed constantly with thoughts of food. We could look great (never great enough) and be afraid it wouldn't last. We saw ourselves as fat, whether we were or not. We never ate a bite of food without thinking it was going to make us fat. Joy and I concluded that if we could think ourselves fat, we could also think ourselves thin. What we focused on was not how fat people got temporarily thin (we knew all about that), but *how thin people stayed thin eating the foods they loved*!

Think for a moment of a friend or a person you have known who is naturally thin. Not dieting thin, not can-eat-only-salads-at-every-meal thin, not a-life-full-of-sacrifice-and-suffering thin, but naturally thin. Someone who never diets and who freely eats anything and everything he or she wants. A naturally thin person is someone who is probably more interested in living and loving than in eating. She doesn't follow convention. Sometimes she eats cake instead of dinner. Sometimes he has a hamburger for breakfast. Sometimes life gets so interesting he even forgets to eat! However naturally thin people eat, they stay thin forever. The Thin Within concept evolved from a comprehensive study of such people.

When we discovered these concepts in the 1970s, they were so innovative that we didn't think anyone would believe us. However, we knew it worked! From the beginning we were committed to keeping the Thin Within principles very clear and to demonstrating complex psychological concepts in understandable terms. In 1979 Joy left Thin Within to get an advanced degree in public health and start a second family. Since then I have continued to develop, expand, and deepen our basic ideas regarding weight mastery. I am now willing to take an unequivocal stand against diets.

A key point is understanding why diets don't work. Consider the following statistics:

• There are 79 million overweight Americans; 40 million are seriously overweight (30 pounds or more).

• Medical and emotional problems associated with obesity and eating disorders (including anorexia and bulimia) have reached epidemic proportions.

• At any time approximately 20 million Americans are attempting to lose weight, spending 10 billion dollars each year on pills, shots, hypnosis, and diet programs.

• The most common nutritional problem of the aged in this country is not malnutrition, lack of a balanced diet, or osteoporosis. It is obesity!

It is clear that diets don't work. They don't work because they're based on a negative focus, one of deprivation, starvation, and denial. It's as if there were a Newton's law of dieting where every action produces an equal and opposite reaction, setting up a pendulum motion within us.

According to the Herman-Polivy study at the University of Toronto, diets actually trigger excessive eating behavior, causing us to *gain* weight. That's right, diets make us fatter—because when we diet we swing back and forth on that pendulum from one extreme to the other. When we're on a diet we're thinking about the forbidden foods and when we finally go off that diet (after enjoying the compliments for a few days) we compulsively eat everything we have been depriving ourselves of. And, finally, diets don't work because they do not take into account the uniqueness of the millions of people who are seriously overweight in this country. I have seen more damage and more heartbreak from dieting than I ever saw from merely being overweight. As Dr. Joyce D. Nash, a Stanford University–trained psychologist, points out, "Ninety percent of formerly rotund people will backslide sooner or later."

To be effective, a weight-loss program must be tailored to you—your life-style, your goals, in response to your body. Thin Within does this. This is a personalized program in which you will discover your own answers. In this book you will find what really works for you and you will never forget it!

What we've done is formulate an entirely new concept in Thin Within, one of harmony and balance. We discovered how to eliminate the pendulum effect—the on and off, deprivation and excessiveness, set up by dieting. This step-by-step process is explained in this book. We'll show you exactly how to eat just enough of the foods you love *and* release all of your excess weight.

Every exercise and tool in this book has been tested by thousands of Thin Within graduates and proven to be effective. Each day builds on the prior ones so that from the very first chapter you will be eating like a naturally thin person. All you'll be doing the rest of the next 29 days is waiting for your body to catch up!

Each chapter contains an interesting, clear explanation of the Thin Within process, accompanied by thought-provoking written exercises and Success Tools that will help you master your weight. The tools I will give you have been used by housewives, executives, athletes, doctors, factory workers, teachers, teenagers, and children.

Thin Within not only contains motivating ideas, exercises, and tools, but also success stories of Thin Within graduates, showing how they apply the Thin Within method to their lives. I will tell you Tanya's story, who not only let go of 10 pounds, but more important achieved mastery over her bulimia-anorexia; Toby Bartholomew who effortlessly lost 70 pounds so fast that her friends didn't recognize her; and Julia Drannan who not only lost the 20 pounds that she'd been and the objective perspective that has brought excellence to this book.

Special thanks to Neal Rogin, my first teacher in the art of writing.

Thank you, Carol Costello, for your expertise in guiding and shaping the foundation of this book and for introducing me to my wonderful agent, Annie Brody, who became an enthusiastic supporter of Thin Within.

Praise to Harriet Bell, my editor, for her invaluable input, excellent guidance, and genuine enthusiasm.

Thank you to Marilyn Crossland and Kasumi Hart for your diligent typing (and retyping) of the manuscript. And many thanks to Susan Strong and Sharon LaBell for their wonderful help in interviewing graduates.

Bouquets of roses to Joan Songer and Kay Lekich, whose support has been unending and greatly appreciated!

And ultimately, I thank God for the strength and courage to share my heart and life experiences with you, dear readers. Accept this book with love!

Judy Wardell

Acknowledgments

I give thanks and appreciation to the twenty thousand Thin Within graduates who have contributed so much to our understanding of eating disorders, who have demonstrated the success of our philosophy, and who have carried the Thin Within concept out into the world.

Thanks to all of the Thin Within staff, whose hearts are filled with so much love for our work and who want to see Thin Within affect the lives of millions.

I would like to thank all of those who have been a part of my life and who have contributed to my personal growth and to the development of the concepts of Thin Within, particularly Ron and Alexandra Siegel, Drs. Arthur Ciancutti and Bruce Fabric, Werner Erhard, Lisa de Longchamps, Alan Dolit, and Pastor Gary Barber.

Thanks to my remarkable parents who have shown me the true meaning of love. They have had unending and unwavering faith in me and have always supported me without question.

My admiration and deepest respect go to my collaborator, Barbara Austin, who was an inspiration to me and who was able to translate the excellence of our workshops onto the printed page.

A special thanks to my talented seminar leaders, particularly Kathi Sims, Sandi Simoni, and Doreen Van Winkle, who have so effectively touched the lives of thousands. Their daily dedication to the Thin Within philosophy, their insights, and their teaching expertise will be forever remembered.

A special tribute goes to the love of my life, Arthur, who was by my side every step of the way with encouragement

Contents

To my dear friend Joy Imboden Overstreet for the conception of Thin Within. I gratefully acknowledge her contribution to this endeavor which has changed the lives and lightened the hearts of thousands.

PUBLISHER'S NOTE: This book contains a weight-loss program for the reader to follow. However, not all weight-loss programs are designed for all individuals. Before starting this or any other weight-loss program you should consult your physician.

The case histories used in the text are based on research and interviews. The relevant facts are real, but we have changed names and other identifying details to respect the privacy of the individuals.

Published by Harmony Books, a division of Crown Publishers, Inc., One Park Avenue, New York, New York 10016 and simultaneously in Canada by General Publishing Company Limited

HARMONY and colophon are trademarks of Crown Publishers, Inc.

THIN WITHIN, An Educational Corporation, is a trademark of Judy Wardell.

Manufactured in the United States of America

Library of Congress Cataloging in Publication Data

Wardell, Judy.
Thin within.

1. Reducing diets. 2. Reducing—Psychological aspects. 3. Reducing—Case studies. I. Austin, Barbara Leslie. II. title.
RM222.2.W276 1985 613.2'5 85-25273

ISBN 0-517-55687-1

Designed by Claudia Carlson

10 9 8 7 6 5 4 3 2 1

First Edition

WITHIN™

How to Eat and Live Like a Thin Person

Judy Wardell

in collaboration with
BARBARA AUSTIN

Harmony Books/New York

struggling for five years to lose (since her last baby!) but started her own business with all the energy she released. Whether your weight-loss goal is 5 or 105 pounds, you will let go of it in the most enjoyable way possible—by eating all the foods you love to eat. This is because at Thin Within we have conclusively established that the key to permanent weight loss isn't *what* you eat but *when* you eat and *how much*.

If you follow the instructions given here with a sincere commitment to make changes, you will, like thousands of other successful Thin Within graduates, revolutionize your relationship to food, eating, and your body.

So treat this book as a safe place where you can tell the truth about yourself—a place where you can be totally honest about food, eating, and your body. Each new Thin Within weight-loss tool will become like a seed that drops in your heart. The instructions and exercises in this book will act like fertilizer, mulch, and weeding to lay the groundwork for a beautiful thin you to flower from those seeds.

My purpose in writing this book is to put these tools into the hands of those seventy-nine million Americans who have food, eating, or weight-related problems. To revolutionize the way we eat from the attitude of "more is better" to eating "just enough" of what our bodies really love. Above all, it is to say emphatically that diets don't work and never will produce long-term success. Thin Within ends the obsessive, heart-breaking problems of eating and overweight. We remove the misery of dieting and put in the wisdom of Thin Within. Thousands of our graduates use these tools successfully every day. They have received these tools by taking Thin Within in its 6-week or weekend version (see page 245 for more information). What a joy it will be to have you join them, manifesting on the outside the magnificence you are on the inside.

Finally, this is a book to read, write in, study, underline, and share with family, friends, and colleagues. If you feel uncomfortable writing in this book, then use a separate notebook, as we do at Thin Within workshops. Thin Within is the truth you have been searching for—a lifetime do-it-yourself guide for freeing yourself from excess weight and keeping it off forever!

THE WHERE-I'VE-COME-FROM QUESTIONNAIRE

The following "Where-I've-Come-From Questionnaire" is a tool to assess your past history and pinpoint where you are now so you can achieve all your weight-loss goals. Read it and circle the appropriate answers. Following Day 29 you will fill in a Where-I-Am-Today Questionnaire, and by comparing your answers you will see how much progress you've made during this process. You'll be amazed!

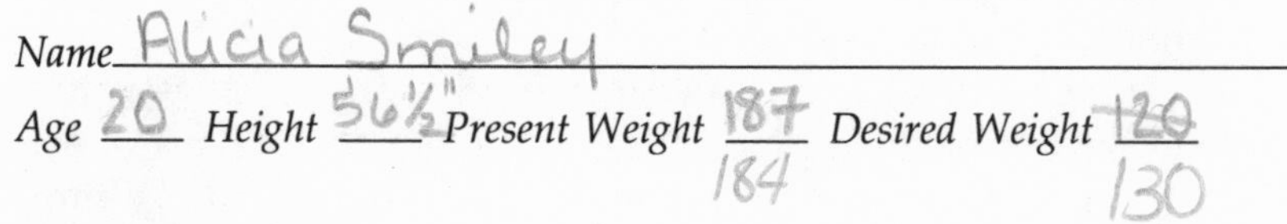

Name Alicia Smiley

Age 20 *Height* 5'6½" *Present Weight* ~~187~~ 184 *Desired Weight* ~~120~~ 130

BRIEF HISTORY:

1. How was your weight as a child? (under 12 years old):

   Underweight
   Ideal Weight
   ✓ Somewhat Overweight
   Very overweight

2. How old were you when you first decided you had a weight problem?

   1–7 yrs
   8–12
   ✓ 13–19
   20–29
   30–39
   40–49
   50–59
   over 60

3. How frequently do you weigh yourself?

   once a day
   2–5 times a day
   ✓ 2–5 times a week
   2–5 times a month
   Very rarely

4. How was your father's weight when you were young?

   Underweight
   Ideal weight
   ✓ Somewhat overweight
   Very overweight

5. How was your mother's weight when you were young?

   Underweight
   Ideal weight
   ✓ Somewhat overweight
   Very overweight

ON THE FOLLOWING QUESTIONS, CIRCLE THE NUMBER THAT BEST APPLIES:

6. How much of the time are you on a diet or sacrificing certain types of foods?

   1 2 3 4 5 6 7 8 9 10
   Always — Never

7. How frequently do you eat foods you really love?

   1 2 3 4 5 6 7 8 9 10
   Never — Always

8. How often do you think of yourself as a thin person?

   1 2 3 4 5 6 7 8 9 10
   Never — Always

9. Can you visualize or imagine yourself at your desired weight?

   1 2 3 4 5 6 7 8 9 10
   Never — Always

10. Do you think you are aware of your body's hunger and fullness signals?

    1 2 3 4 5 6 7 8 9 10
    Never — Always

IMAGINE THAT YOU HAD A FUEL GAUGE FOR YOUR STOMACH, MUCH LIKE THAT ON A CAR, WHICH REGISTERED HOW EMPTY OR FULL YOU WERE:

11. At what point on the gauge do you usually start eating?

    0 1 2 3 4 5 6 7 8 9 10
    Empty — Comfy — Stuffed

12. At what point on the gauge do you usually stop eating?

    0 1 2 3 4 5 6 7 8 9 10
    Empty — Comfy — Stuffed

WHAT ARE YOUR CURRENT CONCERNS?
Rate each item listed below.

13. Spending too much time worrying about your weight or eating behavior?

1 2 3 4 5 6 7 8 9 10
Serious Problem No Problem

14. Weighing frequently?

1 2 3 4 5 6 7 8 9 10
Serious Problem No Problem

15. Anorexia Nervosa?

1 2 3 4 5 6 7 8 9 10
Serious Problem No Problem

16. Bulimia?

1 2 3 4 5 6 7 8 9 10
Serious Problem No Problem

17. Disliking your body?

1 2 3 4 5 6 7 8 9 10
Serious Problem No Problem

18. Thinking too much about food?

1 2 3 4 5 6 7 8 9 10
Serious Problem No Problem

19. Snacking? (between meals or at night)

1 2 3 4 5 6 7 8 9 10
Serious Problem No Problem

20. Alcoholic beverages?

1 2 3 4 5 6 7 8 9 10
Serious Problem No Problem

21. Cigarettes?

1 2 3 4 5 6 7 8 9 10
Serious Problem No Problem

22. Feeling guilty about what you eat?

1 2 3 4 5 6 7 8 9 10
Serious Problem No Problem

23. Eating out of stress or boredom?

1 2 3 4 5 6 7 8 9 10
Serious Problem No Problem

24. Social eating? (parties, restaurants)

1 2 3 4 5 6 7 8 9 10
Serious Problem No Problem

IN GENERAL, HOW DO YOU RATE YOUR LIFE IN THE FOLLOWING AREAS?

25. Health

1 2 3 4 5 6 7 8 9 10
Poor Excellent

26. Energy level

1 2 3 4 5 6 7 8 9 10
Low High

27. Physical activity

1 2 3 4 5 6 7 8 9 10
Sedentary Extremely Active

28. Productivity

1 2 3 4 5 6 7 8 9 10
Low High

29. Job satisfaction (consider student or housewife as a job)

1 2 3 4 5 6 7 8 9 10
Unsatisfying Very Satisfying

30. Close relationships (friends)

1 2 3 4 5 6 7 8 9 10
Unsatisfying Very Satisfying

31. Family relationships

1 2 3 4 5 6 7 8 9 10
Unsatisfying Very Satisfying

32. Sex life

1 2 3 4 5 6 7 8 9 10
Unsatisfying Very Satisfying

33. Ability to speak up for what you want

1 2 3 4 5 6 7 8 9 10
Difficult Easy

34. Level of self-esteem

1 2 3 4 5 6 7 8 9 10
Low High

DAY 1

Weight Mastery

From the moment you complete this first chapter you will be eating like a thin person. This is because what Thin Within offers you is not merely weight loss but the successful Keys to Weight Mastery, which is completely different.

A master is someone who is a professional, the best, and who exercises his or her skill effortlessly with a sense of sureness and serenity. Weight mastery means that you have absolute serenity in your mind, body, and spirit with regard to food, eating, and your weight. It means you know exactly what you need to do in order to achieve balance in these areas. This is exactly what Thin Within teaches . . . the art of thinking, eating, and living like a naturally thin person.

Kathleen O'Brien, a Thin Within graduate who lost 40 pounds said, "Thin Within helped me discover a series of tools inside myself. I didn't have to *learn* them from the outside or buy them. They were there all the time. And consequently, I am never out of control when I eat."

The reason for our success is that Thin Within is the first cybernetic weight-loss system that contains both the *software* (ideas) and *hardware* (thirty-five exercises and tools to implement these ideas) that will enable you, like Kathleen, to utilize your natural ability to solve your own weight problems.

Cybernetics is a comparative study of electronic processes, the nervous system, and the brain. Such studies have given us a more complete understanding of how we learn. Human beings are basically learning mechanisms, and we solve problems and attain our goals, like computers, by using feedback. Thin Within is based on this concept. It has nothing to do with controlling yourself, using will power or domination of any sort.

Each of us has a God-given genius inside that will reveal all we need to know to solve our problems. As Kathleen said, these tools are within you, not somewhere "out there." All you need to do is learn how to tap into your own weight-loss genius. The keys I'm going to give you today will unlock the door to that genius.

In the past, before I realized that what I needed was already within me, whenever I was depressed, sad, or upset about my eating and my body, I used to think if only . . . if only I could find the perfect diet, that would solve everything.

The attraction to a diet is the *promise*. The promise that you will lose 10 pounds instantly. The promise that if you lose 20 pounds you will meet the man or woman of your dreams and get the perfect job, because you're going to be thin and beautiful. However, a diet is a false promise, based on will power, deprivation, sacrifice, and control. After nibbling on salads, mock sour cream, and dry toast, you're finally down to your ideal weight. Your social life picks up. You get those compliments. And what happens? Your will power fails you and you're overeating once again.

Isn't it interesting that Adam and Eve lost paradise because of food . . . an apple? We know this from our lives, don't we? We want to become masters at the dinner table. We know that if we can achieve success with food, eating, and weight loss we can achieve success in other areas as well.

It's interesting too, that food is the only one of our obsessions (drinking, smoking, overwork, sex) that we can't eliminate. We can stop smoking or drinking but we can't stop eating. We need food to survive, so we must learn to handle it masterfully.

A diet is for followers. It's like climbing a mountain with a great deal of suffering, carrying the heaviest backpack possible. Weight mastery means being at the top of the mountain with the perspective and the power that say, "I know what I'm doing. I can eat like a thin person anywhere, anytime. I can do it!" This is what I offer today. It is much more than a hope or a promise! If you use these keys, you will become a master of your weight, loving what you're doing every step of the way.

In this book I will share with you how our Thin Within graduates use these success tools. However, in order for *your* story to turn out a success, it's very important that you don't just *read* this book. Thin Within is a weight-mastery program that is dedicated to producing results. It involves walking the walk, not merely talking the talk. Results come from positive beliefs and actions, in other words from doing this book. So don't be a spectator. Get those marvelous results by participating 100 percent with me. You deserve to have all your heart desires.

So if you're ready and willing, do this: make quiet time for yourself and Thin Within every day. Read and do the exercises as honestly and completely as possible. Dedicate these 30 days to you!

Are you ready to be successful? All right. Congratulations!

Now sign and date this page as a symbol of your commitment to yourself: ______________________

Thank you.

Meister Eckhardt, a theologian, once said that the way to get a perfect circle every time is to put the center in the right place. Our heart is the center of our perfect circle. Your signature on this page is your commitment to begin on your personal weight-mastery project from this new place, *your* center—your heart.

Now we're ready to proceed. The first exercise is extremely important because it will help pinpoint where you are, right now, in your relationship with food, your body, and the way you are currently eating.

MY LAST SUPPER EXERCISE

Slow down for a moment, take a few deep breaths, and take a look at how you usually approach food and eating. Can you remember the last meal you had? Jot down your answers to the following questions. Don't think about your answers too much, simply write down what first comes to mind.

Do you remember what you had to eat at this meal?

What was it?

How did you eat your food?

Did you take plenty of time to enjoy it or did you gulp it down?

Did you like what you were eating?

What was going on in the environment as you ate?

Was there a lot of noise and talking?

Were you reading?

Was the TV on?

Or was your meal filled with peace and quiet so you could really savor your food?

How did you feel as you ate this meal?

Was it an enjoyable experience?

Beans, cheese, tortillas, bread, crackers

I ate fast and too much

I gulped it down

I was watching tv

No

No

No

Yes

No

I felt guilty because I overate and

the food was high in fat

No.

I imagine your experience wasn't too different from the way I used to eat. I was always afraid I wouldn't get enough, always thinking of the next bite as I gobbled down the present one untasted. I ate in my car, standing, and on the run. I grazed when I made dinner for my family or friends. One of my greatest challenges was to see how many things I could do while eating—read a book, talk on the phone, or watch TV. I ate like Anne, a Thin Within graduate, who said "I was always rushing to the refrigerator to gobble down the best leftovers before my older brothers beat me to it." I, too, thought I was in a food race—and I always lost.

One of the basic premises of Thin Within is that naturally thin people do not diet. The tools in this book are the result of a meticulous study of how thin people really eat. In fact, the first tool I'd like to introduce to you will allow you to eat like a naturally thin person starting right now.

THE THIN WITHIN KEYS TO WEIGHT MASTERY

The Thin Within Keys to Weight Mastery are the heartbeat of this book. They are your guide to conscious eating. All you have to do is follow them and you'll melt down to your naturally slim state.

At Thin Within we say that the first day you learn how to do it and the next 29 days you learn to overcome your resistance to doing it. The body doesn't resist. The body loves eating consciously and enjoying every morsel of food! It is the mind that resists. After investing years in the struggle, the mind can't believe the first step is this easy.

We have thousands of graduates who will tell you the Thin Within Keys to Weight Mastery unlocked the door to a palace filled with room after room of riches and an "I deserve to have it all" attitude! For what is the use of having it all if we don't feel we deserve it? As one of our graduates told me, "Thin Within is a precious gift that you give to yourself." You will truly experience this in the next 29 days.

So read each of the following Keys to Weight Mastery carefully. Then copy (or photocopy) them so that you can carry them in your purse or wallet. Hang them up on your refrigerator or anywhere you usually eat, so they can guide you away from compulsive overeating to consciously eating "just enough" of the foods you really love.

THE THIN WITHIN KEYS TO WEIGHT MASTERY

1. Eat only when my body is hungry. This is the fundamental key to weight mastery. We eat only when we're hungry. We feel there's no such thing as a little bit, or *kinda* hungry. We either are or aren't. When in doubt, don't eat. At Thin Within we pay attention to our body's messages. They can be trusted. And if we eat only when we're hungry, we'll lose weight and we'll feel *good.* If you don't have a chance to eat when you're hungry, don't worry; your hunger will go away and come back later. Hunger acts like a snooze alarm. It comes, goes, and always returns. It's even all right to *be* hungry and choose *not* to eat! Now you're probably saying to yourself "but I'm always hungry." Not true! You'll learn on Day 5 how to tell when you are *really* hungry.

2. Reduce the number of distractions in order to eat in a calm environment. At Thin Within we love to eat, and being in a calm environment truly allows us to slow down and enjoy every wonderful morsel of food. We listen to our bodies' messages and we revere our food. For the next 30 days, arrange your life so that you can eat alone whenever possible. This makes it much easier to recognize old eating patterns that don't work and to change them to new workable ones. When we say reduce the number of distractions we mean turn off the TV and the music, send the children out, and put aside reading, etc. You'll learn later how to eat like a thin person with family and friends, at parties and business meals.

3. Eat only when I'm sitting. There is no joy in eating on the run. Such eating is not very satisfying and it encourages picking. It's interesting how when you eat on the run, the mind erases the meal but the body doesn't. If you sit down at the table every time you eat, you will naturally slow down and pay more attention to your food, which is precisely the point. It is an invitation to conscious eating.

4. Eat only when my body and mind are relaxed. Why? Because you will enjoy your food more. It's not necessary to be in a state of meditation—simply spend a moment or two being aware of yourself and the food before starting to eat. Take a few deep breaths. Look at the food before you as though you are seeing it for the first time. You will be amazed at how this slowing-down process will enhance your eating experience.

5. Eat and drink only the food and beverages my body loves. This permission is for you to choose to eat *anything* that you want to eat. In Thin Within there are no good foods or bad foods, no shoulds or should nots. You can eat *anything* your body loves to eat. What do we mean by that? We mean ask your body what it would really love to eat. You do this by closing your eyes, touching your stomach and abdomen, and asking your body, "What would you really love to eat right now?" I know this might be a novel (perhaps even scary) idea to you. However, if you listen to your body, you can trust its answer.

At first as you learn to tune in to what your body really wants, you may hear it say it wants all those "forbidden" foods you never allowed yourself when you were dieting. Go for it—as long as you eat only when you're really hungry and stop *before* you're full. What is happening is an important part of the process. Your body is breaking its "diet pattern" of labeling foods as "good" or "bad," which will allow you to eat like a naturally thin person—when you're hungry and only those foods you love. Practice abandon and at the same time stay attuned to the messages of your body, which can be trusted. It will tell you exactly what it wants in order to feel and function at its best. Don't worry if you think you're eating too many cookies or too much pasta—eventually your body will call out for broccoli.

Begin to notice what you really love and what you don't. For instance, you may think you love a combination sandwich and *your body* really doesn't. Perhaps what you really love in a BLT is the bacon and mayonnaise and not the tomato and bread. Then go for that. If the part of Mexican food you really like is the melted cheese, then have just that. Practice abandon and be creative. Savor all the flavors of your food and drink, and when you eat, enjoy the food without diluting it or washing it down with liquids.

6. Pay attention only to my food while eating. When you're eating alone that will be easy to do. However, when you're with another person, it might seem difficult to pay attention only to your food. When eating with others spend about thirty seconds focused on your food, then put your fork down and focus your attention on the other person and the conversation. I have noticed that I cheat the person I'm with if I eat while conversing, and I deprive myself of the pleasure of my food if I talk while eating. So alternate eating and talking. This will allow you to receive optimum pleasure from the food *and* your relationships.

7. Eat slowly, savoring each bite. It seems obvious, doesn't it, to eat slowly and enjoy each bite? Why then is it so rarely practiced? We rush through life not noticing what we eat, whom we talk to, what we say. We're never really here in the present moment, we're in the future or in the past. By using this key every day—eating slowly and noticing each bite—we are teaching ourselves to be in present time, and we will begin to enjoy more fully all areas of our lives.

8. Stop *before* my body is full! At Thin Within we learn when to begin (when we're hungry) and when to stop (when we've had "just enough"). You'll learn how to tell when you're hungry and when you've had enough on Day 5. This is how you train yourself to return to the natural balance of your body. It's very simple. You start when you're hungry and you stop when you're comfortable. If you begin eating when you're hungry, it will be easier for you to recognize that comfortable place to stop, which is just before you are full.

The best way to incorporate these eight keys into your life is to copy them on a separate sheet of paper and put them on your refrigerator, in your purse, wallet, desk, or wherever you might want or need a gentle reminder.

These Thin Within Keys to Weight Mastery apply to *all the food* you eat and *all the beverages* you drink, *except water*. That includes coffee, tea (even if you drink it black), and diet sodas (drink these only if you love them and you're thirsty). We consider everything except water as food and recognize that everything except water affects our level of hunger.

If you use these Thin Within Keys to Weight Mastery and really become conscious of your eating, miracles will occur in your life. This is not an empty promise. Willa Cather once said that too often we look for others to create miracles for us, when the truth is, "miracles surround us at every turn if we but sharpen our perceptions of them."

Remember: this is not a diet. In fact, if you are currently on a diet—using diet pills, shots, or liquid protein—I ask you to put them aside and give yourself to Thin Within 100 percent. Remember: you can eat *anything* you want and release weight as long as you use the Thin Within Keys to Weight Mastery. And that, my friend, is your first miracle!

SUCCESS TOOLS

• Use the Observations and Corrections Chart below for the next 30 days to observe which Thin Within Keys to Weight Mastery you're using and which ones you're not using. Every time you choose to eat or drink place a check mark or a star beside the key that you used. If there are empty boxes at the end of the day, that will be an indication for you to pay more attention to that particular key.

• Have fun with this chart! Use gold stars or colored pens, knowing that every time you make your special mark you're getting thinner.

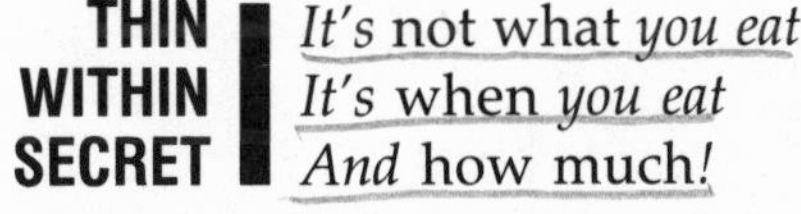

THIN WITHIN OBSERVATIONS AND CORRECTIONS CHART

Observations	Day 1
1. I ate when my body was hungry.	
2. I ate in a calm environment by reducing distractions.	
3. I ate when I was sitting.	
4. I ate when my body and mind were relaxed.	
5. I ate and drank only the things my body *loved*.	
6. I paid attention only to my food while eating.	
7. I ate slowly, savoring each bite.	
8. I stopped before my body was full.	

DAY 2

Coming Home to Your Body

Today I'm going to introduce you to an old friend who has been waiting for you, a friend you have been abusing for a very long time—your body.

Think of the millions of people who are dieting. Think of the abuse we have inflicted on ourselves with pills, shots, fasting, stapled stomachs, intestinal by-pass operations, induced vomiting, and anorectic behavior. I shudder when I think of all I put my body through by being bulimic for one year and having my jaws wired shut for a month.

Toby Bartholomew, a Thin Within graduate who lost 70 pounds, is now so trim that three friends recently failed to recognize her. She used to jog (painfully) four miles at a time when she weighed 235 pounds! Liz Banni, who lost 60 pounds, binged for thirteen years before she came to Thin Within. "I'd be so full I would almost burst," she told me. "I'd lie down on the bed, throw up, fall asleep, and wake up to do it all over again." Barbara Box, who, with five other friends, used to have "Scout's Honor Parties." They called them that because the three fingers used in the Scout's pledge represented to them the three fingers they'd stick down their throats after they had binged all night, drunk gallons of water, and bounced on a trampoline to make themselves vomit.

Your problem with food may not be as extreme as the above, but unfortunately such forms of self-abuse are very common among people with weight problems.

At Thin Within we do not believe that abusive behavior or deprivation in any form is an effective method for permanent weight loss. In fact, as Toby found, you will enjoy food more than ever before in your life.

Thin Within is about freedom. I can now go into any restaurant and pick out all the dieters—they're the ones with the sad, strained faces, eating cottage cheese and carrot sticks. We have an entire generation of men and women with wrinkles around their lips from keeping them painfully shut against all foods they *really* love.

Thin Within promotes eating with pleasure, anything you want, and letting go of the weight you choose to at the same time. It is about loving your body into shape. It is about trusting. Above all, it is about a reconciliation between you and your body.

Toby no longer forces herself to jog. Her body now tells her when it wants to exercise, just as it tells her when and what it wants to eat. What Thin Within did was teach her how to listen to her body.

ALL I DO IS BREATHE

One of our graduates, Sonya Martin, tells about her unnaturally thin sister. Sonya calls her "unnaturally thin" because her sister has to work so *hard* at it, always dieting and exercising. When Sonya told her she was going to take Thin Within, her sister said, "Well, I don't think it will ever work; it's too easy. There's not enough sacrifice, pain, and struggle; it's just too much fun. You can't become slim and enjoy yourself in the process." But Sonya took the workshop and the next time her sister saw her, she had melted down from a size 14 to a size 10. Her sister was flabbergasted! Not only had her sister been dieting for years to maintain her figure but she was doing aerobic dancing four times a week and playing tennis on the weekends.

Sonya told her, "All I do is breathe."

"What?" her sister said.

Sonya said, "All I do is breathe and use the Thin Within

Keys to Weight Mastery and the weight simply melts from my body."

You'll understand what Sonya means as you progress through this book. You will never *have* to exercise again in order to lose or maintain weight, unless that's what your body, your friend, desires. Today is about coming home and reuniting with your body.

MIRROR, MIRROR

One of the ways we formulate ideas about our body is by the reflection we see of ourselves in a mirror. Usually we make a judgment and glance away. Today we're going to observe our bodies in the mirror in an entirely new way.

Stand in front of a mirror without clothes on and slowly observe your body from head to toes, front and back. Remember, I said *observe*—not judge. When you notice your critical mind judging and evaluating what it sees (this is good or that is bad), thank your mind for sharing and continue observing as if you were watching your body on a TV screen.

Do this slowly, looking carefully at each part—go from your feet to your calves to your knees, thighs, stomach, abdomen, chest, shoulders, arms, hands, turn around and look at your buttocks, back, neck, hair, face . . .

The reason you are looking at your body so carefully today is because by the end of this 30-day period, your body is going to change and you will want to have an accurate reading of where your body is right now. Also, this exercise will allow you to begin to learn how to connect with your body without the usual judgments and criticisms (we'll go into this more in Day 4), and to tell the truth about the current status of your body. Don't underestimate the value of this exercise. If you don't have a full-length mirror, borrow or buy one, and do it today so you can get on with your Thin Within way of life. You deserve to see all of you!

Now jot down notes to yourself about what you became aware of as you did this exercise, such as areas of your body you may have been ignoring, things that surprised you, places you'd lovingly like to change.

Observations About My Body in the Mirror Exercise

I observed many things-
My lower legs are nice, my
shoulders are ok, I like my
mouth, ears, and eyes
I would like to change my
stomach, thighs, and back,
and the heaviness I carry
all over that makes me
big!

I love my body now even though
its 50-60 lbs overweight!!
Its soft and loveable and will
get better w/ each pound I lose

This is an invaluable exercise and can become a very helpful tool for you in the next 28 days. Many Thin Within graduates find it helpful to use the Mirror Tool often to keep in touch with their body. Instead of weighing yourself, monitor your progress by looking in the mirror and asking your body how many pounds it has released. It will tell you. It can be trusted.

One woman called me after first using the Mirror Tool and said she hadn't looked at her body full-length in a mirror for over twenty years. She'd been looking only at her face, erasing the rest. Through Thin Within she learned to forgive herself and affirm to her body that she would serve it 100 percent by using the Thin Within Keys to Weight Mastery.

If there is a particular part of your body you want to change, one of the most effective techniques is to lovingly touch that area in order to increase your awareness of that part of your body. For instance, one graduate still hated her thighs even though she had let go of over 40 pounds, wanting them to be smaller and firmer. Every day she looked in the mirror and lovingly touched her thighs. She also did this whenever she took a shower. Today she considers her thighs to be ideal.

However your body looks, remember that it has served you. One of our graduates, Diane Schmidt, works as a men's wardrobe consultant. "I constantly see men buying clothes that are too tight. 'This will make me lose weight,' they say. But the truth is that all it will do is make them feel bad about themselves and cause them to head straight for the refrigerator. I tell them to use the Thin Within approach; to love their body as it is right now."

Imagine for a moment how your body would serve you if you loved it just as it is right now, not after it becomes your ideal, but *while* it's melting down to its natural size?

By looking at your body in the mirror without the usual self-flagellation and judgment, you are beginning a process of communication between your mind and your body that you will find unbelievably accurate and special.

Tamara Blanchard, a Thin Within graduate, said, "Last week I went to a pot-luck dinner and what I really wanted to eat was a piece of chocolate cake and stuffed mushrooms. And that's exactly what I had. During the week I lost 5 pounds and I know just where it came from—my hips! I felt it."

I realize it sounds unbelievable that by having such an intimate relationship with your body you can actually *feel* from where you are losing weight, but this is an everyday occurrence in our workshops.

Today is not merely the beginning of a friendship with your body, it's the beginning of a love affair. Your body is going to experience things in the next 28 days that are so pleasurable and special that it will respond by happily melting down to its natural weight! This is a very exciting day. Your first day of freedom!

SUCCESS TOOLS

• Mark the Thin Within Observations and Corrections Chart for today.

• Use the Thin Within Keys to Weight Mastery every time you choose to eat or drink today.

THIN WITHIN SECRET

Do unto your body
As you would have it do unto you—
The more you love and nurture your body
The more it will love and nurture you.

THIN WITHIN OBSERVATIONS AND CORRECTIONS CHART

Observations	Day 2
1. I ate when my body was hungry.	✓✓
2. I ate in a calm environment by reducing distractions.	✓
3. I ate when I was sitting.	✓✓
4. I ate when my body and mind were relaxed.	✓
5. I ate and drank only the things my body *loved*.	✓✓
6. I paid attention only to my food while eating.	✓
7. I ate slowly, savoring each bite.	✓✓
8. I stopped before my body was full.	✓✓

DAY 3

Creating Realistic Dreams

What would your life be like if it were totally satisfying? Not merely in the areas of weight, appearance, and how you feel but in all aspects of your life. Today we will begin a process which will help you find answers to these questions.

We begin by considering what you'd like your life to be like after this thirty-day Thin Within process. Have you ever asked yourself what the difference is between merely dreaming and experiencing the fulfillment of those dreams? We all have dreams—how we would like to look, the perfect job, perfect relationship, etc. But how can such dreams become real? Dreams become reality when we keep our commitment to them.

Before Thin Within I had no idea about the power of commitment. I often fell into things, drifted along, "hoping." It either worked out or it didn't—I had no idea that the only person limiting me was myself. Now I know that setting goals reveals to me where my true commitment lies. By setting realistic goals I become very clear about what I really want in my life. Then all I have to do is follow whatever steps are necessary to achieve those goals.

Setting goals is like creating a target for ourselves so that we can marshal all our energy to hit the correct spot. At Thin Within we call goals realistic dreams. You now have 28 days left—how much weight do you want to lose? This is your first realistic dream. State it in a positive, result-oriented manner.

Goal #1 I am going to weigh ____ pounds by Day 30.

The second goal is to be concerned with any area in your life which will support your dream of being a naturally thin person. For instance, if you could have your health, fitness, appearance, or environment any way you wanted, what would it be like? Set a goal that you can get really excited about! Again, state it in a positive, result-oriented manner, remembering to watch for duplicates. For instance, if you've stated above that you want to release 15 pounds by Day 30, don't restate that same goal by saying you want to fit into your favorite green dress by Day 30 (which would mean you'd have to let go of 15 pounds to do it!).

Goal #2 I am going to ________________ by Day 30.

For your third goal, ask yourself if you could have any job, relationship, or house you wanted, what would it be? Take a risk. Be adventurous in stating your third goal, remembering, of course, that you have 28 days to achieve it! Pick something that will be exciting and challenging for you to achieve. Besides making your goal positive, specific, and result-oriented, be sure the goal you set is your own, not someone else's good idea for you. When I first decided I wanted a new car, I kept thinking what I *should* get instead of what my heart really *wanted.* Finally I took a risk, which delighted (and scared) me. This mobilized a lot of fresh energy and I decided to get the car of my dreams. . . . It seemed unreasonable and unaffordable, but I did it! The pleasure I now experience every time I drive my car convinced me that the risk was worth taking.

This is a day for dreams. Your imagination and determination will help you achieve them.

Goal #3 I am going to ________________ by Day 30.

By writing down these goals you are programming the marvelous computer of your mind. You're saying, here, this is what I want. And you're saying to your unconscious, you work on it.

One way to facilitate this process is to read over your three goals before going to sleep each night. By doing this you will be putting your goals to work while you sleep. And in the morning you'll discover new ways to achieve your realistic dreams. Plus, you'll feel renewed energy to use the Thin Within Keys to Weight Mastery.

Another way you can help mobilize and direct energy toward your weight-loss goal is by drawing a very clear mental image of how you would like to look. You can do this in your imagination or you can cut out a picture from a magazine. One of the things I did was to take a picture of myself as a teenager (when I was naturally thin) and put it in a place where I saw it daily. I wanted to get back to the freedom of natural thinness and that picture was an incentive for me. Just tape or draw your picture in this book by your goals.

Now restate your three goals below. The reason we have you rewrite them is to have all the goals in one place so you can easily refer to them and also to set them apart because of their importance.

Goal #1 I am going to weigh 167 pounds by Day 30.

Goal #2 I am going to exercise 4x/wk by Day 30.

Goal #3 I am going to join a volunteer group by Day 30.

SUCCESS TOOLS

- Be totally honest with yourself. Slow down and wait until you're hungry. Close your eyes, touch your stomach and abdomen, and ask your body what it would really love to eat. Eat slowly with as few distractions as possible, savor every single bite and stop before you're full.

- Do a loving thing for your body today. Enjoy a sauna, a hot tub, have a massage, get a shave, or have your hair done, go for a walk, have a facial, a manicure, or simply apply lotion to moisten and refresh your skin. Whatever you choose, remember, every time you do a loving, nourishing thing for your body, you're getting closer to that naturally slender you!

- Mark your Observations and Corrections Chart.

- Use the Thin Within Keys to Weight Mastery.

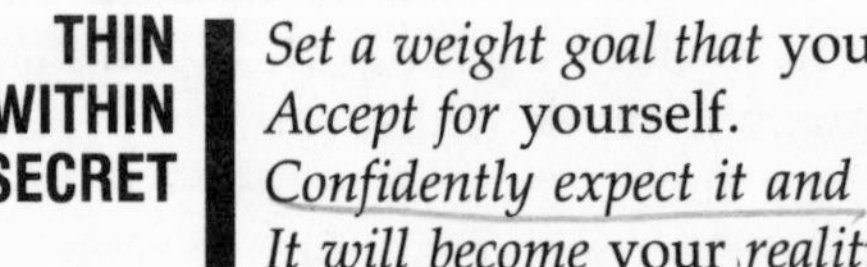

THIN WITHIN SECRET

Set a weight goal that you *believe in and*
Accept for yourself.
Confidently expect it and
It will become your *reality!*

THIN WITHIN OBSERVATIONS AND CORRECTIONS CHART

Observations	Day 3
1. I ate when my body was hungry.	
2. I ate in a calm environment by reducing distractions.	
3. I ate when I was sitting.	
4. I ate when my body and mind were relaxed.	
5. I ate and drank only the things my body *loved*.	
6. I paid attention only to my food while eating.	
7. I ate slowly, savoring each bite.	
8. I stopped before my body was full.	

DAY 4

Winning at Losing

"I get my commitment back even stronger every time I have a slip. My slips actually make me stronger because they teach me about myself," says Connie Carrington, who released 40 pounds.

At Thin Within we say that weight mastery is like a roller coaster, each one of us having our own unique ride with its ups and downs. And the learning experience often doesn't take place when we're riding the crests saying, "Isn't this great?" But rather, it takes place when we slip, slide down into that valley, hit bottom, wake up, and ask, "Hey, what happened?" This is because learning takes place when you start asking questions: "What didn't work here?" "Why not?" "What can I learn from this experience?" If you apply the wisdom learned from one slip, then the next slip isn't quite so traumatic.

PROGRESS RATHER THAN PERFECTION

Some people think that life is supposed to be like a freeway where we just zip along perfectly and expediently without deviation, directly to our goals.

Perhaps when you saw my picture on the back cover of this book you may have doubted that I could really understand *your* weight problem, or that my weight problem was somehow easier to resolve than yours. The truth is that the principles of Thin Within evolved precisely because I had such a terrible time achieving weight mastery. I know exactly what it means to get in your own way. It took me a long time to figure out that I was my own worst enemy. Finally I realized that I alone was responsible for the committee in my head that was constantly criticizing me, and that I alone could determine whether my life would be a success or failure.

One of the things I learned is that even though we may feel certain someone out there is doing it perfectly, the truth is, *no one* is doing it perfectly! And that's exactly how it is supposed to be.

I said in Day 1 that Thin Within works so effectively because it is based on the fact that human beings are cybernetic. This may be defined as the use of information from past behavior to correct and improve present behavior. Do you realize what this means? The only way we learn is by an increasingly educated process of feedback based on trial and error.

Making mistakes is essential because each mistake corrected makes us wiser and moves us closer to the perfection we seek. This is one of our fundamental learning processes.

Sandra Muntz, a Thin Within graduate who has six children, called me one day absolutely thrilled because she had finally understood the roller-coaster concept. That morning she had been hurrying around, getting her children ready for school and all the time thinking of where the cookies were hidden. "I don't hide them from me," she said laughingly. "I hide them from the kids!" As soon as she got her children off, she went to the hiding place, took a cookie out of the package, stopped, looked at it, and realized she didn't even want it. She wasn't even hungry! What she really wanted was a reward because of the frustration of getting her kids off to school! She said, "Don't you see what a triumph this is for me? Two months ago I *was* eating every cookie in sight and today I realized the cause." Now she can correct this undesirable habit with compassion.

The beauty of feedback is that it facilitates progress. It may be three steps forward and two steps back, three steps forward and one step back—yet you will be moving forward. There is value in the ups and downs, the downs being as much or more a part of the learning process as the ups.

And this leads us directly to our next tool. The Observe and Correct Tool will show you how to observe (without judgment) what isn't working, learn from it, and put in a correction to move you nearer to your goal. The sooner you're willing to correct what doesn't work, the sooner you'll reach your weight goal.

THE OBSERVE AND CORRECT TOOL

In Thin Within we say life doesn't consist of right or wrong, success or failure. Life is about using the information learned from what works and what doesn't work to move us toward our goals. You keep getting feedback and putting in corrections to make your progress more efficient.

The key is to be able to learn from being in the down part of that roller-coaster ride so you can put in the proper correction and move upward. How can you do this without judging and criticizing yourself?

Take a few deep breaths and imagine that you're watching yourself eating on a television screen. The reason we want you to view yourself on a screen is that by doing so you will attain a much needed perspective. You can't change your behavior if you can't see it. By imagining your behavior on a television screen, you achieve the distance you need to correct it. You can use this in all areas of your life, but today we'll focus on food, eating, and weight mastery.

Now let's say that today when you got up you hurriedly went to the cupboard and gulped down six cookies before you even started breakfast! You weren't thinking about the Thin Within Keys to Weight Mastery at all—you were eating unconsciously. Now ordinarily, if you saw yourself eating like this, you'd be your own worst critic. FATSO! you'd think. Here you go again! You'll be fat forever! Ugly! No one loves you! You're hopeless!

The problem with this kind of judgment is that it is self-defeating. I know because I used to do the same thing. It was as if I were on a football field all by myself and I was tackling, tripping, banging into myself—nobody else was there! That's the pain of constantly judging and evaluating ourselves. And, of course, it makes us feel miserable, battered, and abused. And what do we do? *We eat more!* Judging ourselves never works—it just adds to our overeating.

The study at the University of Toronto by psychiatrists Herman and Polivy that we mentioned earlier showed that when dieters feel they have "blown it" it sets up a what-the-heck effect. In other words, by eating those six cookies you beat yourself up unmercifully, then say, "Oh, what the heck, I've blown it, so I may as well continue overeating today. Tomorrow I can start dieting again."

In Thin Within we eliminate the what-the-heck effect by eliminating judgment. Instead, we give you the Observe and Correct Tool. Next time, instead of judging and evaluating yourself on that TV screen, take a few deep breaths, observe what isn't working (eating six cookies unconsciously), and put in the correction (simply wait until you're hungry). If your body tells you at that time it wants cookies, go for it—eating only until your body has had just enough.

There's no shame and no blame in this approach. It is merely observing your behavior as objectively as you can (that's why we use the television-screen method), giving yourself feedback (oh, that isn't moving me to my weight-loss goal), and putting in the correction. Hmmm. What will work? Let's see, Key #3. Next time, instead of standing and gulping down the cookies, I'll sit down, and slowly enjoy savoring one cookie at a time until I reach that place called comfortable.

From time to time as you go through this 30-day process you may observe your old judgmental mind wanting to take over. At these times you might experience feelings of being on an uncontrollable roller-coaster ride. When you feel you are in the downswing of that ride, don't panic. Just observe what isn't working and put in the appropriate correction that will move you toward your weight goal. The sooner you observe what isn't working and put in the corrections—without judgment—the sooner you'll be at your desired destination.

One of our graduates, Sally Dartmouth, told me how her job as a manager has turned around since she has used this Observe and Correct Tool. Now when she talks to her people, she doesn't dwell on what's wrong or how they failed. First of all she asks them what's working. And then she asks them what isn't working and what corrections they can put in to change that.

The Observe and Correct Tool will give you a tremendous sense of freedom. If you ate one time when you weren't hungry, all you have to do is observe your behavior on that TV monitor and say, "Oh, that didn't work. I'm not going to release weight if I eat when I'm not hungry." The correction you will put in is not to eat next time until you're hungry. Simple as that—no harsh words and no heavy hand.

At Thin Within there's no weighing in, no blame or shame. No one, including yourself, is going to judge or evaluate you. What we're striving for is a reconciliation between separated friends—your body and your mind. You've had enough abuse. It's time for love and support. Thin Within is a safe place, a home, for you to tell the truth about what you're doing with food and eating. By doing so you can resolve your weight problem once and for all.

SUCCESS TOOLS

• From this day on, when you look at your Thin Within Observations and Corrections Chart, you'll be looking at it from the point of view of what works and what doesn't. Here's how it works using the Observations and Corrections concept. The boxes with the fewest checks mean you're not using that particular key enough. So you, as a self-correcting instrument, receive this feedback and put in your own correction. "Oh, I ate three times yesterday but only sat down once. That's why I counted only one meal." So make sure you're sitting the next time you eat and you will progress more rapidly.

THIN WITHIN SECRET

Life is a roller coaster
And we can change every down into an up
By observation and correction
In the present moment.

THIN WITHIN OBSERVATIONS AND CORRECTIONS CHART

Observations	Day 4
1. I ate when my body was hungry.	
2. I ate in a calm environment by reducing distractions.	
3. I ate when I was sitting.	
4. I ate when my body and mind were relaxed.	
5. I ate and drank only the things my body *loved*.	
6. I paid attention only to my food while eating.	
7. I ate slowly, savoring each bite.	
8. I stopped before my body was full.	

DAY 5

The Only Scale There Is

One of our graduates who lost 60 pounds was convinced after an introductory session at Thin Within that she could do it on her own. The concepts of eating only when you're hungry and stopping before you're full seemed so obvious. She went home, promptly binged, and finally admitted she needed help. "Why," she said, "I discovered I don't even know what hunger is!"

Today's tool, the Hunger Scale, will teach you how to recognize when you are hungry and when you've had "just enough." Many of us have difficulty in defining and interpreting our bodies' messages, and the Hunger Scale will greatly facilitate this process. It is a powerful way to help you learn to consult the very best authority on weight mastery—your own body.

WHAT IS HUNGER?

If you're like most of the participants in the Thin Within workshops, you have little idea what hunger is. Some people say they are always hungry. Others equate hunger with being poor or feeling unloved, and want to avoid it at all cost. Some will stay on a "diet" *only* as long as they don't experience hunger! Yet, since childhood our bodies have been sending us accurate hunger messages day after day, even though we usually ignore them.

I remember my own experience as a child. I was active and energetic and I'd be hungry by 4 P.M. when I got home from school. I really didn't want to snack then—I wanted dinner. But I always had to wait until 7 P.M. for dinner when my father came home from work. So what did I do? I sneaked food in the afternoon and then had to clean my plate at dinner even though I wasn't hungry!

What we're going to do today is an exercise that allows you to get in touch with your genuine hunger level—that hunger we experienced in childhood that resulted in our eating *only when we were truly hungry.* Do you remember your first bite at those times? To me it tasted like heaven.

First, read this exercise to get the gist of it and then go through it for yourself. It would also be very helpful to put this on tape.

DISCOVERING MY OWN HUNGER LEVEL EXERCISE

What I'd like you to do is sit in a straight-back chair, take everything off your lap, and take a few deep breaths.

Now focus your attention on your *teeth.* Then focus your attention on your *mouth.* Are there any sensations in that area that you would call hunger? Any messages that say it is time to eat? Or just comfortable? Or full? Can you tell the difference? Are you thirsty?

Now focus your attention on your *throat.* Are there any sensations there that you would call hunger? Time to eat? Comfortable? Full?

Now focus your attention on your stomach, the area just below your rib cage. What sensations do you experience in this area? With what do you associate these sensations?

Now move your attention to your abdomen. Put your hands on your abdomen and rub it a bit. What sensations do you experience there? What do you associate these sensations with? Are you hungry? Are you thirsty? Are you comfortable? Are you full?

Now rub both hands on the entire area of your abdomen and stomach. Okay?

On a scale of 0 to 10—0 being empty, 5 being comfortable,

and 10 being stuffed, at what level of hunger is your body right now? Write down that number . . .

And on a scale from 0 to 10, 0 being unpleasant, 5 just okay, and 10 feeling terrific, how do you feel right now? Write down that number . . .

Do you notice any relationship between your level of hunger and your state of being?

All right—good work!

THE HUNGER SCALE TOOL

The information you derived from doing the preceding exercise regarding the degree of hunger you experience can conveniently be illustrated by the following, which we call the Hunger Scale:

Stuffed	10
Comfortable	5
Empty	0

Remember that 0 is empty, 5 is comfortable, and 10 is stuffed . . . you know, Thanksgiving-stuffed—aching-belly-have-to-lie-down-on-the-sofa—can't-eat-another-bite-or-it-will-ooze-out—stuffed.

At Thin Within when we say that we eat only when we're hungry and stop before we're comfortable, we mean 0 to 5 eating. We feel there's no such thing as "I'm just a little bit hungry." You're either at a 0 or you're not. And if you're not, *don't eat.* Understand that one of the things we're going to be doing during the next 25 days is bringing your Hunger Numbers into clear focus. It may take some time to accomplish this; however, it will happen.

The exercise you just did is an excellent way to clarify your hunger levels at all times. You are to check in with your body to determine your hunger level any time you consider eating. Wherever you are—at a restaurant, your desk, the dinner table—take a few deep breaths and focus your attention first on your mouth, then your throat, and then finally, actually touching your stomach and abdomen, with your eyes closed, ask it, "Where am I on the Hunger Scale *right now*?" and listen for your *body's* response. Beware of the mind, which may give you conflicting information at these times! You must learn to trust your body. Closing your eyes helps to lower the focus from your head down to your body, from which you'll get a much more accurate response.

Sometimes you may be surprised to find that you're thirsty rather than hungry; that your body does want something, and what it wants is some cool, refreshing water.

Always remember that the essence of Thin Within is: Eat only when hungry—at 0.

WHEN IN DOUBT, DON'T EAT!

If you eat 0 to 5 or less you will release the weight you want to lose. And if you continue to eat 0 to 5, you will maintain your ideal size—whatever that is *for you* for the rest of your life. Don't worry about getting too thin. At a certain point your body will stabilize at a size that is appropriate for you. The reason for this is that your body sends moment-by-moment messages of what it requires and what it wants. Listening to your body and eating 0 to 5 is the way to be in teamwork with it. The Hunger Scale is based on this fundamental principle: the ultimate authority on weight mastery is your own body.

This process works! You'll begin to enjoy the light, energetic feeling of 0 to 5 eating. Instead of listening to everyone else about your weight problems—doctors, teachers, parents, dieticians, nutritionists, coaches—listen to the wisest authority of all—your body!

THE BODOMETER PROCESS

Today you have received a tool that is readily available and asolutely infallible. At Thin Within we call it the Bodometer Process, which is the method used to receive a present-time reading from your body. No matter where you are, take a few deep breaths, close your eyes, focus on your body, feel your abdomen, and ask yourself these questions:

Am I hungry?

What is my Hunger Number right now?

How much weight have I released?

How much do I weigh?

Without giving it too much thought, simply allow your body to give you the answer. Trust it, for it's an essential key to your weight mastery.

THE HUNGER SCALE AS A TOOL FOR WEIGHT MASTERY

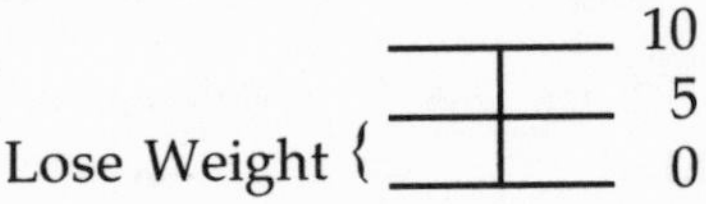

10
5
Lose Weight { 0

If you eat 0 to 5 or less, you will lose the weight you targeted on Day 3.

You can also choose to stop eating at any point below a 5. This will certainly hasten your weight-mastery process. Carla Benton released 15 pounds in two weeks, while eating 0 to 3. You can also choose to ride your 0 for a while and enjoy being hungry. (I did say *enjoy*—what a novel thought!)

Remember that hunger is like a snooze alarm that goes off and on. It's like a tap on the shoulder. "Oh, I'm at a 0. But I'm having too much fun to stop and eat! I'll just wait." It goes away and will come back again with another gentle tap.

Having permission to eat when you're hungry also means having permission *not* to eat. Think about that! It means allowing yourself to ride that zero as you happily progress a bit faster toward the goal you want. That's entirely up to you. You are your own coach in this weight-mastery game. What we're doing today is making sure that you and your body are on the same team!

Just remember: eat 0 to 5 or less and your body will melt down to its own natural slimness and absolutely stay there for the rest of your life. If this sounds unbelievable, test it out for yourself. I feel you will quickly become convinced!

If you start eating when you're at a 3 and eat to a 7, then you'll stay overweight. You won't lose weight or gain, you'll merely maintain the extra weight that you're carrying around right now.

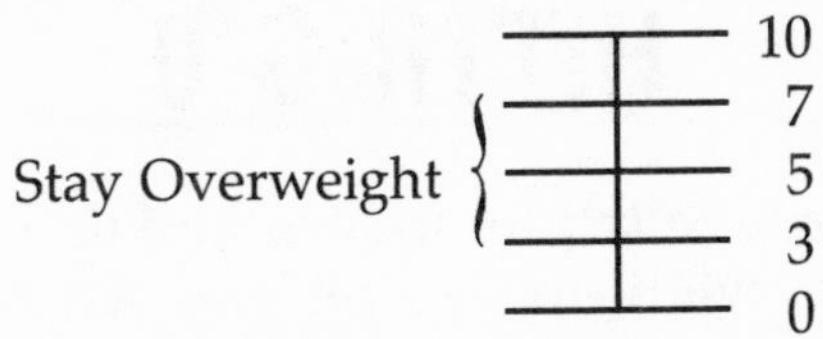

And obviously if you eat from 5 to 10 you'll gain more weight. This level of eating is what you may have been doing before you picked up this book.

0 to 5 = You'll melt down to your natural size and maintain it for the rest of your life.
3 to 7 = You'll stay overweight as you are right now.
5 to 10 = You'll gain weight.

Gain More Weight { 10, 5, 0

HOW OBSERVATION AND CORRECTION WORKS

The best way to tell if your Hunger Numbers are accurate is by the results you're getting (or not getting). If you're releasing weight you must be eating 0 to 5. So whenever you use the Mirror Tool, ask your body how many pounds it has released. Remember, the more you communicate with your body the more it will give you proper feedback! Adjust your numbers accordingly. If you seem to be maintaining an undesired weight or gaining more weight, then you are not eating 0 to 5. You can lower your numbers by slightly reducing your intake and remembering to eat the foods your body loves! The more you are willing to experiment, the more it will work for you. Don't give up and think that you're different or that you don't understand. After all, it may have been some time since you listened to your body! Have patience as you familiarize yourself with all the fine tuning of 0-to-5 eating, remembering that perseverance is the key to your success.

HITTING 0

Finally, if you're having trouble hitting 0, here are a few suggestions that will help you get in touch with your 0 and speed up your weight-mastery process. This is for the courageous ones.

• This evening don't eat. Experience hunger.

• If you do eat or drink this evening, have only one item you love. Yes, *anything* you would love to eat or drink. Eat below or up to a 5, use the Thin Within Keys, record your intake, and ask yourself this question—"Will I love myself more if I eat or drink this?"

• Drink only liquids in the morning—water, milk, juices, teas, coffee, something your body would enjoy—and use the Thin Within Keys to Weight Mastery.

• Make a fist with your hand. Now hold it up in front of you. Do you know what your fist represents? Your fist is approximately the size of your stomach when it is empty. Because your stomach is an expandable organ it can stretch to accommodate all the 5 to 10 (or more) eating you've ever done. So, the next time you're at a 0 and before you start to eat, hold up your fist! It will be your friendly reminder of how little food is actually required to bring your body to that place called comfortable.

SUCCESS TOOLS

• To help you clarify your Hunger Numbers, here is an extremely helpful Success Tool, the Food Log. This is a chart on which you're to write down all your Hunger Numbers before and after eating, and record every single bite that you eat for the next 20 days. Does this sound like a lot to ask? Well, it is. However, it will be worth it!

Everything counts, every bite, lick, sip, everything you eat or drink except water (coffee and tea included).

Remember, every bite counts, and if you are wondering who's counting, the answer is—*your body*.

This is a chance to come out of hiding and tell the whole truth about your eating. It's a chance to observe what you're doing so that you can put in any corrections that may be necessary. If you go out to eat and you don't have your Food Log with you, write your food items on a napkin or in a notebook and record them in the Food Log as soon as you can. Also check in with your body before looking at the menu by closing your eyes and asking your body where it is at that moment on the Hunger Scale. Keep this Food Log up to date. It's a very important Success Tool. You're observing when and how much you eat and you're getting in touch with your hunger level.

THIN WITHIN FOOD LOG

Hunger #	Time	Item	Amount
0	Noon	Peanuts	Handful

• Continue to mark your Observations and Corrections Chart. If you need more room, please add paper to this book. Do it *no matter what.*

• Use the Thin Within Keys to Weight Mastery.

THIN WITHIN SECRET

In Thin Within
We count hunger numbers
Instead of calories!

THIN WITHIN FOOD LOG

Hunger #	Time	Items	Amount
0	10:09	wheat roll, raisins	1, 2
0	1:00	wheat roll, cheese, corncob	1, 2oz, 1
2	2:30	M+Ms	1pkg
2	6:30	fun fruits	1pkg
2	8:30	chips, 1/2 quesadilla	

THIN WITHIN OBSERVATIONS AND CORRECTIONS CHART

Observations	Day 5
1. I ate when my body was hungry.	
2. I ate in a calm environment by reducing distractions.	
3. I ate when I was sitting.	
4. I ate when my body and mind were relaxed.	
5. I ate and drank only the things my body *loved*.	
6. I paid attention only to my food while eating.	
7. I ate slowly, savoring each bite.	
8. I stopped before my body was full.	

DAY 6

Fat Machinery

For the next 4 days we're going to take a close look at the subject of Fat Machinery. One of the most significant breakthroughs in my study of eating disorders came with the thorough understanding of this concept. Before Thin Within I tried diet after diet, and yet I could not completely or permanently free myself of 38 extra pounds. And yet there were times when I could eat anything I wanted and not gain weight. I just couldn't understand the difference between my fat days and my thin days.

I'd come home from a five-course dinner (starting with snails baked in garlic butter and ending with chocolate decadence) with an inexplicable craving for more. It was more than an empty feeling (God knows I was stuffed to the brim). It was as if there were a crater-sized emptiness inside of me which nothing could fill. Food wasn't the answer, but I didn't know where else to turn. I'd walk into my apartment, go straight to the kitchen, and get a loaf of bread. You'd think if I were going to binge at least I'd choose something interesting! I'd eat toast, with butter, grape jam, or peanut butter on it. I didn't even enjoy it, but I felt compelled to do it over and over until I became so nauseated I could make myself vomit. Have you ever felt like that?

I didn't know it at the time but I was eating entirely out of my Fat Machinery. Fat Machinery can be defined as unconscious or automatic eating that is triggered by external stimuli or internal programming. Webster's defines a machine as "the means by which something is kept in action," or "a system of organized activities which perpetuates or carries on a process."

Thin Within's definition of a human machine is one who responds to stimuli without intelligence. It's as if we become machines around food, switched on by outside stimuli and unable to turn ourselves off. Suppose you're walking down the street and smell doughnuts. This may trigger an automatic response, "I love doughnuts," so, even though you're not hungry, you find yourself buying doughnuts. That is Fat Machinery at work.

Before Carol Donohue came to Thin Within she used to binge while her husband worked the night shift. She'd go into the grocery store and buy a gallon of ice cream, a loaf of bread, a dozen doughnuts, and an assortment of nuts, candy, and cheese. She'd go home and eat and eat until it was all gone and then pass out. When her husband came home, he would find all her empty cartons, wake her, and say, "You wanted to get caught, didn't you?"

The truth is, we desperately want to be caught. We want the seemingly endless cycle to stop.

In the next few days you're going to begin to learn how to turn off your own Fat Machinery so that it will no longer run your life.

FOUR TYPES OF FAT MACHINERY

The next 4 days will be adventures in self-discovery as you'll identify the Fat Machinery that drives you to eat.

1. Conditioned or habitual responses. On Day 7 we'll come to terms with those responses that drive us to eat. For instance, an habitual response I have had predictably occurred when I went to visit my parents. I would walk in the front door, say "Hi, Mom" and immediately find my hand in the cookie jar. I'd see my mother and father and I'd want to eat.

2. Beliefs. On Day 8 we'll talk about the beliefs that we internalize about food, eating, and our weight. For instance I used to believe that I had to eat a big breakfast, a decent lunch, and a satisfying dinner to be healthy. This may be appropriate for people with strenuous jobs, but I thought it applied to everyone, including myself. I paid no attention to the demands of my life-style and my body. I ate like I was a hired hand even though I was doing sedentary work. Since Thin Within I've come to see how this belief hasn't supported me and I now eat only when I'm hungry, which may be once a day, three times a day, or not at all!

3. Past stories. These include all those experiences and situations which have influenced our eating and weight problems. Understanding these dynamics was a real breakthrough for me and I'll share a dramatic personal example of this with you on Day 9.

4. Failures. We'll deal with all the past problems we've had "trying" to lose weight, more specifically diets. Diets deal with the symptoms and never with our Fat Heads. They don't deal with those habitual responses to food that cause unconscious eating. Using the Thin Within tools you will be able to recognize the *causes* of your unworkable eating habits and the *origins* of your Fat Machinery.

I should say at this point that the Thin Within Keys to Weight Mastery are not based on behavior modification, which attempts to redirect actions or substitute one form of behavior or food for another (yogurt for ice cream) without regard to the reasons behind such eating behavior. Rather, you will learn direct, practical methods to correct these old habits, and, during the process, your new, Thin Self will emerge.

AN EXERCISE IN TRUST

Trust is a vital part of all meaningful relationships. It is the act of putting aside our logical mind and flowing with an inner feeling of faith—without the comfort and complete assurance that we're making the correct choice.

Now, I'm going to ask you to participate with me in an exercise that will demonstrate *your* trust. What I'd like you to do right now is to throw out your bathroom scale. Yes, I said throw it away! You may think I'm mad to ask such an outrageous thing! You may say "How will I know if I've lost weight?" "How can I get through the day without stepping on the scale?" "I'll feel lost without knowing *exactly* how much I weigh." My answer is that with the Bodometer Process, which was explained on Day 5 you now have an internal scale that will give you a totally reliable measure of your progress as you melt down to your naturally thin shape. Suffice it to say that when you eat properly according to your Hunger Numbers and are tuned in to your body's messages, you will know precisely how much weight you are releasing.

Your bathroom scale is another example of Fat Machinery. Suppose you get out of bed in the morning and jump on the scale first thing. It says, "You've lost weight" and you say, "Whoopee, I feel great. I can reward myself"—what better way than to have your favorite hot fudge sundae or whatever delights *you*. Or, suppose it's "Oh, no, I've gained four pounds." Immediately you feel depressed, and what better way to deal with depression than—of course—heading straight for the ice-cream parlor to *indulge*! Either way you've failed by letting something other than your own body dictate your feelings and your eating.

To me, the ultimate scale story is the time I went to visit a friend and found she had her foot in a cast. She had kicked the scale and broken her toe! Your scale may not have been "responsible" for a broken toe, but it may have been responsible for a broken heart and it has certainly not been a supportive feedback system for you.

One of our Thin Within graduates, Bob Corey, explains, "Staying off the scale was the key for me. It's a simple but very logical idea. Now I tune in to my body and listen to how it feels. With the scale I was usually depressed, but even when I was encouraged it didn't necessarily tell me what I needed to know. I lift weights, which adds pounds, but the weight has shifted from my stomach to my chest. A scale can't measure that. Now I go by how I look and feel."

Your daily weight may indeed fluctuate, but you can trust your body to tell you the truth as to when it is at 0 and what it wants to eat. And if you stay in communication with your body, it will also tell you exactly how much weight you've released.

RELEASING AND LETTING GO

You've probably noticed that I rarely say "lost weight." "Losing" something implies that we must find again, or that something unfortunate has occurred. In Thin Within we "release" our excess weight, or we "let it go," forever. It is new language for expressing true and lasting freedom.

From now on whenever you want to check in with your body, instead of jumping onto that Fat Machinery scale, just close your eyes, feel your stomach and abdomen, and ask how many pounds have been released. Trust its response! This may seem like an unusual way to check in with your body, however, I've found the more I did this exercise the more reliable it became!

THE MIRACLE OF THE BLUE SKIRT

Recently one of our graduates, Gloria Burns, told me about what she calls "the miracle of her blue skirt." It seems she had put it on a few weeks ago and it was a little tight. Instead of getting depressed over the thought that she had gained weight, she just put the skirt back in the closet and wore another one. Then she reviewed the Thin Within Keys to Weight Mastery and renewed her commitment to her realistic dream. Within a few days she was able to wear her blue skirt again. This is a perfect example of the cybernetic approach to weight mastery. Observing and correcting without judgments, evaluations, or self-flagellation! The miracle is that the Thin Within tools made it so easy!

At Thin Within there is no judgment. Instead we rely on an easy, gentle system of our body's feedback that continually gives us the information needed to correct unworkable habits. So if you didn't have the courage to throw out the scale on my first recommendation, you have another chance. Do it now! I find in the workshops that those people who are willing to throw out their external scales get in touch with their internal scale more easily and more accurately. Keeping that bathroom scale affirms that the body cannot be trusted.

I also recommend that you throw out any other examples of Fat Machinery that might be lying around the house—diet pills, laxatives, diet books, diet food, and anything else that has to do with deprivation or weight-loss approaches that don't work. Get rid of them! Remove those silly Fat Machinery quotes like: SHE WHO INDUGLES—BULGES or TASTE MAKES WAIST or OVERWEIGHT IS OFTEN JUST DESSERTS that are taped to your refrigerator. All of these are absolutely antithetical to the Thin Within way of life.

All of us have a built-in alarm system. It may appear to be different for each of us. However, when examined closely there is a fundamental similarity. We call *our* built-in alarm system Fat Machinery, however, there is Time Machinery, Money Machinery, Alcohol Machinery, Smoking Machinery, Workaholic Machinery, etc. Whenever we want to avoid something, procrastinate, or generally hide from someone or something, we turn to our familiar machinery, usually our Fat Machinery, and indulge! We do this instead of speaking out, dealing with, or directly handling the situation. So when our Fat Machinery gets turned on its like a red flag . . . oh, oh, something is going on. It may seem like a curse, at first glance, and it is if we continue to ignore it. Like an alarm it gets louder and more annoying. However, when we begin to listen, to understand, and to respond to it, it ceases to be a curse, and becomes instead a blessing, for it goads us to face the truth.

SUCCESS TOOLS

Throw out your scale. I know this is a challenging request, but I know you can do it! If you are hesitant to do this ask yourself these questions: "Has it worked for me so far?" "Have I mastered my weight or food-related issue having the scale?" Write about your experience of letting go of your scale in the space provided below.

Letting Go of My Scale

The scale sort of affirms
my progress. Not weighing
will be very hard. I will
weigh once a month
so I know the #'s

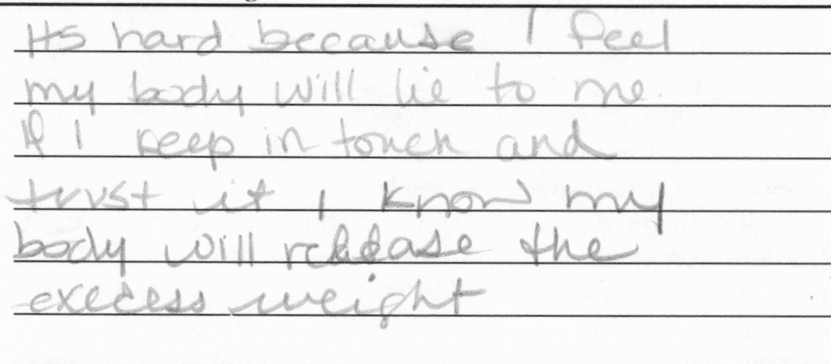

• The more you talk about Fat Machinery the more aware of it you'll become. Point out to others and to yourself how the media trigger unconscious overeating.

• Continue to keep your Food Log. Remember to record every sip, lick, drink, and bite. Write it down even if you ate one peanut!

• Continue to use your Observations and Corrections Chart.

• Use the Thin Within Keys to Weight Mastery.

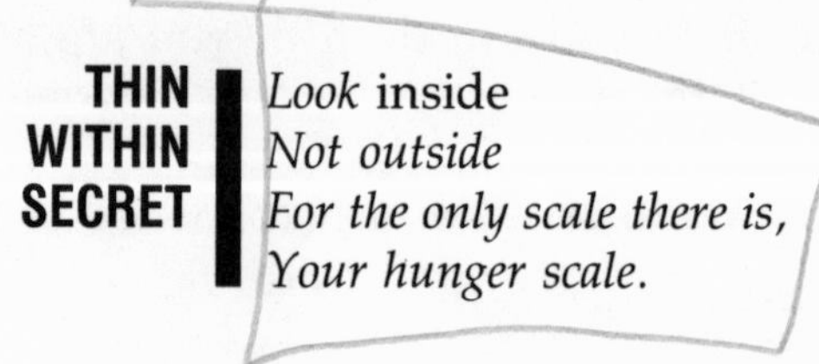

THIN WITHIN SECRET

Look inside
Not outside
For the only scale there is,
Your hunger scale.

THIN WITHIN FOOD LOG

Hunger #	Time	Items	Amount
1	10:00	1 roll, wheat	
3	12:00	2 cups vegis 1 cup crunchnmunch	

ate way too much!

84 1/4

THIN WITHIN OBSERVATIONS AND CORRECTIONS CHART

Observations	Day 6
1. I ate when my body was hungry.	X
2. I ate in a calm environment by reducing distractions.	X
3. I ate when I was sitting.	XX
4. I ate when my body and mind were relaxed.	
5. I ate and drank only the things my body *loved*.	XX
6. I paid attention only to my food while eating.	
7. I ate slowly, savoring each bite.	X
8. I stopped before my body was full.	X

Wait until you are hungry.
Eat a "fistful"
Exercise!

DAY 7

The Making of My Fat Habit

Kathy Downing, one of our graduates, tells how she learned about Fat Machinery as she was growing up. Her mother died before Kathy was one year old, and since her father was in the Navy, relatives took care of her. They were all from the "feed 'em and make 'em happy school" and they used food to compete with each other for Kathy's attention and love. In Kathy's eyes the grandparent who gave her the best chocolate sundae was her favorite! "Even to this day whenever I want to feel better my first thought is to go have a hot fudge sundae!" Kathy's response is an example of a conditioned or habitual response to food that is triggered by seeing or smelling particular foods or being in a certain setting that produces a desire (sometimes overwhelming) to eat even though we may not be hungry.

Today we're going to look at some of the situations in your own life where you may discover similar patterns of Fat Machinery.

FAT AS A HABIT EXERCISE

First, look at the situations or states of mind in the left-hand column below. Let's take the first one and imagine that you're "angry." Close your eyes and recall a time when you were angry. What food or drink do you want when you're feeling angry? Perhaps your answer is pretzels. Then ask yourself "How do I eat pretzels when I'm angry? One at a time? A whole handful at once while pacing back and forth?" Or perhaps you quickly shove them into your mouth while standing in the kitchen or watching TV. Whatever *your* response, write it down in the appropriate column. This exercise is most effective if you move through it very quickly. Don't try to figure out the "correct" answers—whatever pops up in your mind is correct. Just read the situation or state of mind in the left-hand column, then fill in the other two columns with the first thing that comes to mind. The same food or drink may come up more than once.

FAT AS A HABIT EXERCISE

Situation or State of Mind	Food or Drink	Manner of Eating
Angry	Pretzels	Standing in the kitchen; one at a time; slamming the door shut between handfuls
Bored	Sugar, cookies, candy	mindless eating in front of tv
Overwhelmed	mexican	lots in front of tv
Tired	——	
Sick	popsicles	in bed
Depressed	sugar	in front of tv
Tense, anxious	in resturaunt	
Frustrated		
Lonely, unloved	anything	large quantities
Unexpressed anger		
Self-hate, disgust		
Guilt	more of what I was eating previously	

Procrastinating	something I have to cook	
Indecision		
Feeling insecure		
Busy	whatever is around	
Excited		
Having fun	healthy	
Reward		
Luxuriousness	Belgian Lion	slow, enjoyable
Feeling secure		
Family holidays	careful	
Remembering mother		
Remembering father		
Remembering any important figure in your life		

Now look over what you have written. Notice any patterns that appear. See if you can recognize any of your Fat Machinery in action. Do you see how often you eat because of your feelings? Or because you don't want to do something? Or when someone hurts you? Do you sneak food? Eat in your car? In bed? Do certain people trigger a desire in you for certain foods? Do you see how fat could result from your responses to recurring situations? How some eating patterns could become habits?

I know how it used to be for me. As I said, my Fat Machinery popped up every time I walked in the front door of my parents' house. Also whenever I finished a frustrating or upsetting conversation I wanted to head straight for something sweet. Now when such a situation arises I recognize the obvious signs of my Fat Machinery. Knowing what it is and how it works allows me to make the proper correction *so that it will lose its power over me.* All our responses to people, emotions, or situations that turn on Fat Machinery have to do with the past, and yet they influence our present eating.

What does Fat Machinery have to do with 0 to 5 eating? Absolutely nothing! When you eat 0 to 5 you're making present-time choices based on what your body tells you it wants. You may be aware of your Fat Machinery but you don't respond to it by eating. Do you see how important it is to observe and correct? We all have Fat Machinery, however, mastery over it will occur only when we're able to deal differently with recurring situations that formerly produced undesirable eating responses. As one of our graduates said, "You observe the Fat Machinery (because it doesn't go away), identify the trigger, and just let it flutter on by. It's not worth eating over it!"

THE REASONS WE OVEREAT

It's very important that we recognize a variety of eating patterns. Do any of these seem familiar to you?

Worry-wart eating

Preventive eating (I might get hungry later so I'll eat now)

Nervous nibbling

Tourist eating (it may be my last chance to have an eclair)

Eating because it's there

Eating out of happiness, sadness, etc.

Pleasing-the-hostess eating

All of these responses come from our Fat Machinery rather than our body's hunger messages.

Why do we eat like this? What kind of a belief could exert such a powerful influence over our eating behavior? The answer finally came to me after working with thousands of people from all walks of life. Before I reveal this secret let me list some beliefs that "prevent" us from reaching and maintaining our ideal size:

I get weak if I don't eat three meals a day.

I have too many business lunches.

I come from a family of big eaters.

I've always been heavy.

Everyone in my family is overweight.

I could never stop eating ice cream.

I have to attend too many social events.

It will take too long.

I don't look good if I get too thin.

What I'm saying is that underneath all of this is a subtle but powerful belief that holds the key to your freedom. It is: *"I don't deserve to be thin!"*

Your initial response to this may be "Oh yes, that's true for me—I didn't realize it until just this moment!" or "That doesn't apply to me; I know that I want and deserve to be thin, so she must be talking about someone else." You may say that you have a terrific life, a successful career, a wonderful spouse or relationship, lots of friends, and obviously if you have all that you deserve to be thin as well. I understand that you feel you have the right to be at your ideal size—and you do! It is your birthright to be that slim, svelte size you've always dreamed of being. However, wanting to be thin and recognizing a very subtle undercurrent belief of "I don't deserve" are totally different.

It is rare to find a person whose life is 100 percent perfect. I know mine isn't—is yours? We all have imperfections. We all strive for greater fulfillment and a more complete relationship with ourselves and with others. I believe that because of these imperfections we tend to judge ourselves to be unworthy—unworthy of being thin. Being overweight may be used to fuel this feeling of unworthiness. One of the most exciting things you'll learn how to do with this book is change the "I don't deserve" to "I do deserve."

TURNING OFF YOUR FAT MACHINERY

The next time you get upset and head for the refrigerator and you know you're not at a 0 but you want that old familiar blanket of food, ask yourself these three questions:

Am I really hungry?

What is my Hunger Number right now?

Do I want to avoid my feelings by eating when I'm not hungry or do I *really* want to be thin?

These questions are invaluable tools to put in your Thin Within toolchest and are to be used whenever you are faced with your Fat Machinery. The process of mastery over your Fat Machinery may be challenging at times; however, answering the above questions honestly will free you to make choices that support your long-term life-enhancing goals.

SUCCESS TOOLS

• Keep a log to record Fat Machinery every time it pops into your life. The more conscious you become of how Fat Machinery lurks everywhere, the more effective you will be in the mastery of it. If you find yourself going to and from the cupboard or refrigerator looking for "something" to eat; or when your car automatically stops at your favorite ice-cream parlor every time you "try" to drive by; or when thoughts of certain people make you want to eat (for instance, when I think of my friend Carrie I think of pizza!), write down each experience as it occurs. Then ask yourself what those incidents have to do with 0 to 5 eating; the answer is nothing! 0 to 5 eating is asking your body if it is hungry right now, what it would love to have, and then eating or drinking that to a comfortable 5 or less.

FAT MACHINERY LOG

Today write down any Fat Machinery that comes from within you ("I paid for it so I should eat all of it"), from others ("Don't get too thin"), and from the media. As your awareness of Fat Machinery increases so will your feelings of *I Deserve!* As you observe your inner and outer world of Fat Machinery you will experience a greater sense of strength that comes daily from this new insight.

Fat Machinery in Me	Fat Machinery in Others	Fat Machinery in Media
I paid for it...	your fine just the way you are	resturaunt commercials
Its 12:00... Lets eat	you dont weigh more than me	I ♡ Lucy makes me hungry
I'm bored		
trying to avoid work		
tranquilizer		
I've started it so I may as well finish it so I'm not tempted to eat it later		

throw it away / salt it

None of the above has anything to do w/ 0-5 eating and that is what I live by!

To slow down your Fat Machinery and bring it into full view, put up a few signs on the refrigerator or cupboard to interrupt your unconscious responses. Signs like "Am I really hungry?" or "Do I want to avoid my feelings by eating when I'm not hungry or do I really want to be my natural size?"

Continue keeping your Food Log.

Use your Observations and Corrections Chart.

Use the Thin Within Keys to Weight Mastery.

THIN WITHIN SECRET

If you're not hungry
And you want to eat,
It's a sign that
You're avoiding something
Or that something in your life
Is not supporting you.

THIN WITHIN FOOD LOG

Hunger #	Time	Items	Amount
0	12:00	Roll, mayo, peperocini	
2-3	2:00	Crunchmunch	1/2 box
6	3:00	Pop rice	1/2 bag
2	8:30	Salad	

eating to avoid work, tranquilzer

THIN WITHIN OBSERVATIONS AND CORRECTIONS CHART

Observations	Day 7
1. I ate when my body was hungry.	X
2. I ate in a calm environment by reducing distractions.	
3. I ate when I was sitting.	XXX
4. I ate when my body and mind were relaxed.	
5. I ate and drank only the things my body *loved*.	
6. I paid attention only to my food while eating.	
7. I ate slowly, savoring each bite.	X
8. I stopped before my body was full.	XX

DAY 8

The Making of My Fat Head

One day a naturalist was passing by a farm. He glanced over at the chicken yard and noticed among the chickens pecking away at the corn one of the most beautiful eagles he had ever seen.

He said to the farmer, "What in the world is that eagle doing in the chicken pen?"

The farmer drawled, "Well, I really don't know, but I think he thinks he's a chicken. He's been there for a long time and he won't leave. I've tried to scare him away, but he won't go."

The naturalist smiled and said, "I'll make him leave." So he went into the pen and lifted up the eagle. The eagle was indeed a magnificent bird. He flexed his huge wings, and the naturalist could see some of the eagle's latent power.

The naturalist said to the eagle, "Stretch forth your wings and fly! You're not a chicken, you're the king of all birds! You can soar over the entire country. Don't be satisfied with this chicken pen!" But the eagle plopped down from his arm and went right on pecking for corn just like all the chickens. For days the naturalist kept coming back and putting the eagle on his glove. But the eagle wouldn't budge.

Finally, exasperated, the naturalist went back to the farmer. "What in the world can I do? That eagle won't budge. He believes he's a chicken."

"We-ll," the farmer drawled, "if I were you, and I had the time, I'd teach 'im to fly."

The naturalist stared at the farmer for a moment or two. "You know—that's a good idea!"

So the naturalist put the eagle in a cage in his truck and drove to the base of a nearby mountain. There he strapped the cage to his back and climbed high up on the mountain. He set the cage down on a cliff and opened it, but still the eagle wouldn't budge. He just peered out, blinked, and gazed down at the chickens, far below.

The naturalist carefully took the eagle out of the cage and put him on a rock. The eagle looked up at the sky and again his beautiful wings gleamed in the sunlight as they stretched out just a little. For the first time, it seemed that the eagle actually felt different. When he glanced down at the chickens his wings trembled.

The naturalist knew the eagle desperately wanted to fly. He believed that the only thing that stood in his way was fear. So he reached out and very gently pushed the eagle, but it wouldn't budge. He tried again but still the eagle wouldn't move. Finally, the naturalist sat down, utterly exasperated. He looked at the eagle and at the sky and at the chickens far below. "How can I teach him to fly?" he wondered. Then he happened to glance up at the mountaintop, and he knew the answer. He got up, put the eagle back into the cage, and climbed to the top of the mountain.

There the eagles roosted. They built their nests and mated, and soared magnificently.

The eagle saw all of this. And as soon as the naturalist took him out of the cage, he stretched his gorgeous wings and eagerly lifted himself off the rock. At first he dropped but then he suddenly found, like the other eagles, that he could fly effortlessly. The eagle never returned to the chicken yard. He discovered who he was—an eagle. And he loved it.

NATURAL EAGLES

The dilemma of the eagle is very much the same as the dilemma of those of us who believe we're fat when, actually, inside we're all naturally thin.

You are an eagle in this weight-loss adventure. You deserve to fly, you deserve your freedom.

The story of the eagle (retold from the original by Jerry Frankhauser) beautifully illustrates what actually creates our Fat Head, or chicken mentality. It is our beliefs.

The first thing to know about beliefs is that they are self-fulfilling prophecies. If you believe you're a chicken, then you'll not only act like a chicken, you'll be a chicken. If you believe you're an eagle, then you'll be one.

The second thing this story points out is the power that beliefs have to trigger our Fat Machinery. Just as the eagle was limited by his belief that he was a chicken, you, too, are limited by all the beliefs you have about food, eating, and weight loss.

For instance, if *you* believe that chocolate is always fattening, then it will be fattening for *you*. The connection between our beliefs and our Fat Machinery is very important.

Third, beliefs are rooted in the past. They have nothing to do with eating from 0 to 5 in the present time.

And, finally, beliefs distort our understanding of the present. Because the eagle believed he was a chicken his perception of reality was distorted. He saw the world through chicken eyes. He was surrounded by chickens with chicken beliefs. He acted like a chicken, so he was a chicken.

UNWORKABLE BELIEFS

Any belief that results in eating when you're not hungry does not support being that naturally thin person you really are.

An example of this sometimes occurs in hypoglycemia, or low blood sugar. A Thin Within participant, Lillian Barber, complained that she was unable to lose weight because her doctor insisted she eat six times a day to maintain normal blood-sugar levels. By using the Thin Within tools and eating only two meals a day plus half a bran muffin at other times, when she was truly hungry, she released 22 pounds by the end of the six-week workshop. She was ecstatic, as was her doctor. Naturally, if you have a health problem of any kind, it is important to consult with your physician before making any changes in your eating patterns.

Fat Machinery includes those beliefs that work against us. Beliefs such as eating three square meals a day, including certain food groups with every meal and eating everything on your plate, drive your Fat Machinery and therefore have not worked in your best interest in your weight-mastery process.

On day 19 you'll see how to change unworkable beliefs into beliefs that do work. But for today, we're going to heighten your awareness of all those beliefs that are triggering your Fat Machinery.

In the space provided, make a list of all the beliefs about food, eating, and weight loss you have accumulated from your parents, relatives, teachers, books, television, doctors, newspapers, and friends. Allow about three minutes for this exercise. Remember at Thin Within a belief is anything the mind thinks is true.

My Beliefs About Food, Eating, and My Weight

- eat a balanced diet
- eat at least 1,000 cals a day
- dont get too hungry or it will turn to fat.
- clean your plate
- dont waste

I know you already have enough beliefs of your own, but here are some beliefs that you may have and didn't recognize. Do any of these sound familiar?

I get headaches or become dizzy when I don't eat.

I have to clean my plate.

Chocolate makes me feel better.

Starch is fattening.

Once I eat one potato chip, I won't be able to stop.

I need caffeine to start my day.

Eat three square meals a day.

I always gain weight during the holidays.

Losing weight is difficult.

People should like you whether you are fat or thin.

If I paid for it, I'll have to eat it.

If I refuse the food, they'll think I don't like them.

I always gain weight back after I lose it.

If I lose weight I'll be sickly.

I couldn't be thin forever.

I'm fat because I love food and like to eat.

I can't possibly be thin and love food the way I do.

The only way to lose weight is to stop eating.

Never skip a meal.

Never let yourself get hungry.

If I was fat as a child I'll be fat as an adult.

Fat means prosperity.

Dieting is the only way to lose weight.

It's my metabolism.

I'm a compulsive overeater.

I'm a chocoholic.

PRESENT-TIME EATING

The point here is to take a new look at *all* the beliefs you have been carrying around with you. Do you see any contradictions? (Example: I have to start my day with a cup of coffee, but coffee is bad for me.) Do you see any beliefs that have worked for you? Any that have worked against you? Our beliefs are very powerful and yet extremely subtle at times—so subtle that we tend to accept them as facts rather than recognize them as beliefs. So consider letting go of your beliefs at this point. Now you may say "Wait a minute—I can't do that—some of those beliefs are 'true'!" I realize you may be very attached to some of these beliefs. However, true or not, believing I was an ice-cream freak didn't serve me. I eat ice cream today and love it, but I no longer hold that former belief and this frees me to pass an ice-cream parlor and not go in! Instead of eating a quart, I now have a scoop or two of my favorite flavor—Häagen-Dazs coffee—and savor each bite with delight.

Another common belief is that it is okay to gain excessive weight during pregnancy, despite abundant medical evidence to the contrary. To take a Weight Mastery program during this special time might seem most unusual, however we have had many women participate in Thin Within *because* they were pregnant. What a wonderful time to get more in tune with your body! We have found that the Thin Within approach of listening to the messages of your body and eating 0 to 5 uniformly results in less weight gain, more comfortable and enjoyable pregnancies, and happier mothers and babies!

AN ENVIRONMENT OF DISCOVERY

The naturalist thought he could convince the eagle that he was not a chicken simply by telling him the truth. But it didn't work. The eagle had to discover it for himself. What the naturalist *could* do was set up an environment for the eagle to make this discovery himself.

That's exactly what is happening to you. This book is a place for you to discover *for yourself* those beliefs that are keeping your Fat Machinery in place. You'll learn to discard or replace those beliefs that don't work and to create powerful new beliefs in their place—beliefs that support your Thin Self, to eat only when you're hungry and to stop *before* you're full.

You are an eagle in this weight-loss adventure. In the next 22 days you will discover, as have thousands of Thin Within graduates before you, that the entire universe is your domain.

MAKING CHOICES

The next time you're headed for that ol' malt shop, not because you're hungry but because you're feeling bad and your Fat Machinery has been triggered, here's a fourth question to ask yourself (see Turning Off Your Fat Machinery in Day 7 for the other three): "Besides eating, what other options do I have?" In other words, what other diversion can you choose that would serve you? You can exercise, read, go to a movie, call a friend, clean out your closet, write a letter, take a long walk, pick flowers, take a nap . . . the list is endless.

SUCCESS TOOLS

• Make a list of creative options you can choose instead of eating—and do them!

• Keep adding to your Fat Machinery Log. List all of the beliefs you know of—yours, other peoples', from TV, radio, any form of advertising. Remember that these beliefs have a powerful influence on our eating behavior. Don't ask yourself if a belief is right. Ask yourself if it works!

• Continue to keep your Food Log, carefully checking your Hunger Number before you eat.

• Use your Observations and Corrections Chart.

• Use the Thin Within Keys to Weight Mastery.

THIN WITHIN SECRET

You have to let go
Of what you thought you were
To discover what you really are.

FAT MACHINERY LOG

Today write down any Fat Machinery that comes from within you ("I paid for it so I should eat all of it"), from others ("Don't get too thin"), and from the media. As your awareness of Fat Machinery increases so will your feelings of *I Deserve!* As you observe your inner and outer world of Fat Machinery you will experience a greater sense of strength that comes daily from this new insight.

Fat Machinery in Me	Fat Machinery in Others	Fat Machinery in Media

THIN WITHIN FOOD LOG

Hunger #	Time	Items	Amount

THIN WITHIN OBSERVATIONS AND CORRECTIONS CHART

Observations	Day 8
1. I ate when my body was hungry.	
2. I ate in a calm environment by reducing distractions.	
3. I ate when I was sitting.	
4. I ate when my body and mind were relaxed.	
5. I ate and drank only the things my body *loved*.	
6. I paid attention only to my food while eating.	
7. I ate slowly, savoring each bite.	
8. I stopped before my body was full.	

DAY 9

The Making of My Fat Story

During the last 3 days, we've uncovered many things that have contributed to our Fat Habits and Fat Heads. Now we're going to look at how our past stories can affect our eating. Our past can have a profound effect on our present. This concept is very meaningful to me because of a significant experience in my past that resulted in a sudden change from naturally thin to fat. In retrospect, this incident was the traumatic event that sparked my personal and professional interest in weight mastery. It was a breakthrough for me when I realized how my Fat Story profoundly influenced my eating. However, before I share my experience with you, we're going to spend a few minutes going over *your* story. We'll do this by looking at four major events in your life that may have had a significant influence on your eating.

SIGNIFICANT TIMES

This exercise includes a list of seventeen events that may have influenced your relationship with food and eating. If we've failed to list an event of crucial importance for you, please add it. Complete this exercise rather quickly and let the answers surface as you move along.

Pick four from the list and place them in order of the earliest incident to the most recent one in the spaces provided below. An incident may appear on your list more than once.

1. First sexual encounter
2. Fell in love
3. Failed relationship
4. Sexual trauma
5. Moved away from home
6. New job
7. Married
8. Infidelity
9. Pregnancy
10. Abortion
11. Having or raising children
12. Got divorced or separated
13. Major illness (yours or another person's)
14. Lost job
15. Major relocation
16. Disappearance of someone close to you
17. Death of someone close to you

Once you have written down your answers, take a moment to reflect before you proceed with this exercise. Close your eyes, breathe deeply, then let your mind go over the four significant times in your life. Let each incident roll by and simply notice what comes to mind. Now open your eyes and answer the questions by filling in the blank lines.

Significant Time #1 ____________________
Where were you? ____________________
Who was with you or around you? ____________________
Was there a shift in your weight as a result of this incident? ____________________
What decisions did you make as a result of this incident? ____________________
Did your self-esteem increase or decrease? ____________________

Significant Time #2 ____________________
Where were you? ____________________
Who was with you or around you? ____________________
How did you feel? ____________________
Was there a shift in your weight as a result of this incident? ____________________
What decisions did you make as a result of this incident? ____________________

Did your self-esteem increase or decrease? ______________________

Significant Time #3 ______________________
Where were you? ______________________
Who was with you or around you? ______________________
How did you feel? ______________________
Was there a shift in your weight as a result of this incident? ______________________
What decision did you make as a result of this incident? ______________________
Did your self-esteem increase or decrease? ______________________

Significant Time #4 ______________________
Where were you? ______________________
Who was with you or around you? ______________________
How did you feel? ______________________
Was there a shift in your weight as a result of this incident? ______________________
What decision did you make as a result of this incident? ______________________
Did your self-esteem increase or decrease? ______________________

EATING BECAUSE OF OUR STORIES

Now go back and read over your answers. Did you lose or gain weight as a result of the situation? Do you see how eating because of your story is as much Fat Machinery as eating because of a schedule (it's noon—time to consume!)? Or because your scale says you're thin today and you want to celebrate?

Fat Machinery is one of the ways we become overweight, since it is not 0 to 5, present-time eating. I know. I gained 38 pounds because of a traumatic incident that triggered my Fat Machinery. When I was twenty I left home in eastern Oregon to go to dental school in Portland. I was studying to be a dental hygienist, fell in love with a medical student, and became pregnant. I made a decision then that I wouldn't make today, however, it seemed like my *only* choice under the circumstances. I decided to have an abortion. After that experience I felt so terrible about myself and so undeserving that I retreated from all friends and family. I moved to Los Angeles, a place where I'd be anonymous, and began to overeat. Until then I had been quite slim. Eventually I covered my naturally thin body with 38 extra pounds and my spirit sank with thoughts of "I don't deserve."

Those significant incidents you focused on can have profound influences on your eating by strengthening the "I don't deserve" inside of you. And every time we judge or criticize ourselves for not quite making the grade we add fuel to the fire. The end result of all this is incredible self-punishment—all because we see ourselves as undeserving!

But what does the past have to do with the present or present-time eating? Absolutely nothing! Present-time eating is asking our body if it is hungry and eating from 0 to 5 or less, eating the foods we love.

So look at your list of significant times again and understand that those times are past. Keeping them alive will only trigger your Fat Machinery and adversely affect your present-time eating. In order to live and eat in the present time once again I had to forgive myself and those involved in the drama of the past, to bless it, to let it go and move on! You, too, can choose between your past stories and freedom from your Fat Machinery. Even though it may seem painful or even impossible at times, you can do it because what's on the other side is freedom—freedom to fly like that eagle!

SUCCESS TOOLS

• Some of our graduates have found it very helpful during the Thin Within process to keep a *feelings journal.* For instance, I'm sure feelings come up for you as you look back over your Fat Story. We fuel our Fat Machinery with our feelings too, so become more conscious of them by recording them. Remember, the person we tend to be the hardest on is ourself. We tend to be our own worst critic, so be compassionate with yourself and set yourself free from the grips of your Fat Machinery by forgiving yourself.

• Continue to keep Fat Machinery Log. This is your last day!

• Continue to keep your Food Log with your Hunger Numbers.

• Continue marking your Observations and Corrections Chart.

• Use the Thin Within Keys to Weight Mastery.

THIN WITHIN SECRET

Set yourself free
From your Fat Machinery
By forgiving yourself.

FAT MACHINERY LOG

Today write down any Fat Machinery that comes from within you ("I paid for it so I should eat all of it"), from others ("Don't get too thin"), and from the media. As your awareness of Fat Machinery increases so will your feelings of *I Deserve!* As you observe your inner and outer world of Fat Machinery you will experience a greater sense of strength that comes daily from this new insight.

Fat Machinery in Me	Fat Machinery in Others	Fat Machinery in Media

THIN WITHIN FOOD LOG

Hunger #	Time	Items	Amount

THIN WITHIN OBSERVATIONS AND CORRECTIONS CHART

Observations	Day 9
1. I ate when my body was hungry.	
2. I ate in a calm environment by reducing distractions.	
3. I ate when I was sitting.	
4. I ate when my body and mind were relaxed.	
5. I ate and drank only the things my body *loved*.	
6. I paid attention only to my food while eating.	
7. I ate slowly, savoring each bite.	
8. I stopped before my body was full.	

DAY 10

The Weight of Failure

Today you'll experience new ways to get rid of the weight of failure and guilt so that you truly experience freedom and lightness from within your heart. First, let's take a few moments and go back to the day when you went into a bookstore and bought this book. You may have thought you were alone. Actually you were carrying a huge bag full of all the diet failures you've ever had. Wherever we go we carry all the times we took shots or pills and failed, tried diet after diet and failed, or exercised and failed. Also in that sack are all the foods we've eaten that we associate with our failures such as doughnuts, ice cream, cookies, pizza, french fries, etc. And you *always* carry this bag stenciled FAILURES with you, not only as you read this book, but when you're interviewing for a job or meeting someone for the first time. Everywhere you go you're carrying this extra heavy weight. And it's very tiring. It is constantly adding to that feeling of "I don't deserve."

We feel that we don't deserve to be thin because we're bad, we can't make the grade, we can't cut it. We're just too weak-willed to stay on a diet. Look at all the times you've failed. And as a reminder you have your bag stuffed and overflowing with your failures weighing you down.

GETTING RID OF PAST FAILURES

If we believe we're failures, it becomes a self-fulfilling prophecy. We're like that eagle who stayed on the ground with the chickens. If we believe we're failures, we'll act as if we're failures, and we'll fail.

That's why the concept of, "Well, I'm doing the best I can. I'm trying . . ." is so destructive. It's in between. It's hedging our bets against success so when we don't make it we'll be able to say, "Well, I only said I would try!"

Take this book and set it on a table or the floor. Don't touch it. Now, try to pick it up. No, no, no . . . don't *pick* it up. If you pick it up, you're actually doing it and no longer "trying"—just *try* to pick it up. No, no, no . . . now you're not picking it up at all. You see, there is no such things as "trying." You either do it or you don't.

You either are eating something or you're not eating it. Have you ever *tried* not to eat something? Have you ever tried not to eat four chocolate bars in a day? You either did it or you didn't do it! You're either hungry or you're not. You're either at 0 or you're not.

Trying is having a great story about something but not doing it. "Try" is a back door, an escape hatch.

One of Thin Within's workshop leaders talks about how she used to meet every noon with her diet group at work. All they talked about was how the diet they were currently on wasn't working. And Dotty was the most vociferous about it. Of course she never mentioned the chocolate brownie sundae that she was sneaking out to eat every night after a huge supper!

All you have to do to be a success at releasing all the weight you desire is drop that big bag of failures. Just let it go.

You can choose to eat because of those past failures or you can choose present-time eating. Choosing present-time eating means that you simply wait until you're at a 0 (empty), ask your body what it would love to eat, and thoroughly enjoy eating that item to a comfortable 5 or less.

Here's the secret: Your body doesn't care about your

story. I realize it may be painful to hear that, but your body really doesn't care about how you enrolled in a weight-loss program three times (the last time under an assumed name) and failed. Nor does it care about all the doughnuts and chocolate-chip cookies you've eaten in the past. What it does care about is that you are loving, nourishing, and listening to it in the present time.

Here's another secret: If you live in the present then you're not a failure. You're a success! Living in the present means simply observing your behavior with compassion and correcting immediately—no pain, no strain, and no story!!

GETTING RID OF GUILT

All we have to do to get rid of guilt associated with past unsuccessful eating patterns is to eat in present time. You simply wait until you're at 0, touch your stomach and abdomen with your eyes closed and ask it what it really wants to eat. If your body feels it wants a doughnut then go for it! Practice abandon. Go out and get the most spectacular doughnut you can find—one that suits you perfectly! Sit in your favorite spot and savor each delicious bite, stopping when you're comfortable (at a 5 or less).

You see, in present time, there is only this doughnut. And this doughnut doesn't know about all the previous doughnuts in your big bag called "failures." It doesn't know or care about your past. So in present time it's great to eat a doughnut if you're at 0 and that's what your body really wants. Enjoy it and savor each and every bite, and if it takes only three bites to satisfy your body, then throw the rest away.

In this book the weight of failure flips over and becomes the light energetic feeling of eating 0 to 5, which represents successful present-time eating.

You never have to eat because of guilt again. You have permission to eat *anything* your body loves. Isn't that fantastic?

SUCCESS TOOLS

• Do a loving, supportive thing for your body today. You deserve it. You have just dropped a twelve-ton weight off your back! Massage your body with wonderful lotion, get a shave, a pedicure, or take a walk under the trees in the beautiful outdoors. Do something that delights your body.

- Be sure to throw away all those diet books and any other Fat Machinery that reminds you of a diet.
- Keep up your Food Log and your Hunger Numbers.
- Use your Observations and Corrections Chart.
- Use the Thin Within Keys to Weight Mastery.

THIN WITHIN SECRET

Guilt is the most fattening thing there is.
Living in the present
Is the most thinning thing
There is.

THIN WITHIN FOOD LOG

Hunger #	Time	Items	Amount

THIN WITHIN OBSERVATIONS AND CORRECTIONS CHART

Observations	Day 10
1. I ate when my body was hungry.	
2. I ate in a calm environment by reducing distractions.	
3. I ate when I was sitting.	
4. I ate when my body and mind were relaxed.	
5. I ate and drank only the things my body *loved*.	
6. I paid attention only to my food while eating.	
7. I ate slowly, savoring each bite.	
8. I stopped before my body was full.	

DAY 11

How I Successfully Created My Fat Self

Before starting today's exercise, let's review the goals you wrote on Day 3. If you're releasing weight, that's great! If you aren't, your Hunger Numbers need to be lowered a bit. Observe and correct every step of the way. The three hints on Day 6 will help you speed up your process.

The key is 0 to 5 eating. Any time you eat above a 5 all you need to do is put in the correction and get back on course.

Remember, your goals must be realistic. Will you succeed in the next 19 days at the weight-loss goal you set for yourself? If you feel you will, then rewrite that goal in the space provided. If not, make an adjustment that is true and achievable at this time. Do the same for goals 2 and 3. The point here is to be successful!

Date:________________________

Present Weight:__________________

Ideal Weight:____________________

Goal #1________________________________

Goal #2________________________________

Goal #3________________________________

It is most important that you accept the concept that *only you are ultimately responsible for your weight problem.* In the past three days we've seen how old habits, conditioned responses, past ideas and stories can trigger our Fat Machinery and send it into high gear. And we've also seen how past failures and relying on scales can cause or perpetuate weight as a problem. Today we are going to look at how you actually created your weight problem.

HOW I CREATED MY FAT SELF EXERCISE

Answer the four questions below as spontaneously as possible, without getting sidetracked by your stories. Simply state the facts. Spend approximately two minutes on each question. This is the place to get rid of those secrets you haven't wanted anyone to know. You will find as you reveal these untruths about food, eating, and your weight that your naturally Thin Self will joyfully emerge.

1. What I don't want people to know that I did to get fat. . . . The more I lied and sneaked around about my eating the fatter I got. We're only as fat as our secrets. So in the next two minutes record some of your secrets. All those things that you did to get bigger and bigger. The things you did like sneaking cookies in the middle of the night, or professing to be eating practically nothing, overlooking the midmorning and midafternoon snacks of doughnuts and candy bars.

____

____

____

____

2. What my weight problem has kept me from being, doing or having. . . . Do you blame your weight for career failures? Relationship failures? Lack of friends? Disappointing sex life? How did your weight problem keep you from getting that terrific job or a new boyfriend or girlfriend?

____

____

____

____

3. The advantages of being overweight. . . . What has been your payoff? (We don't do anything unless there's a payoff.) What has your weight problem been a solution to? Did you get out of certain tasks? Sympathy from friends? An excuse to see the doctor frequently? An excuse for avoiding certain social functions? Testing people to see if they sincerely cared for the real you rather than just your body? A procrastination technique (I'll do *that* when I get thin). Do you use your weight as the scapegoat rather than face the real issue?

____

____

____

____

4. How I've succeeded in spite of my problems. . . . Despite being overweight you've had many successes in your life. Share some of them here.

____

____

____

____

BLOSSOMING IN PRESENT TIME

You did a fabulous job in creating your weight problem, didn't you? All of the secrets, sneaking, and hiding. The time and money spent "trying" to get rid of it. It's been the focal point of your existence—every hour of every day—what to eat, what not to eat, what to wear, where to go, which friends to see, whom to avoid, perhaps even medical problems (or, at least, worrying about your health).

Has it been worth it? Does your weight problem support you and nourish you in the present time? Are any of the "payoffs" or "rewards" from overeating worth the price you are paying? *The answer can only be no!* Now is the time to start using your new tools to let go of your Fat Self and to facilitate your blossoming into a naturally thin beauty.

You may find it difficult and even somewhat sad to discard the things from which you fashioned your Fat Self. However, the days ahead will be exciting and rewarding, so have courage and proceed!

SUCCESS TOOLS

• Do something thoughtful and special for your body today to demonstrate how much you love yourself. You're always a success when you love your body.

• Continue to observe and correct and mark your Observations and Corrections Chart.

• Keep your Food Log and Hunger Numbers.

• Use the Thin Within Keys to Weight Mastery.

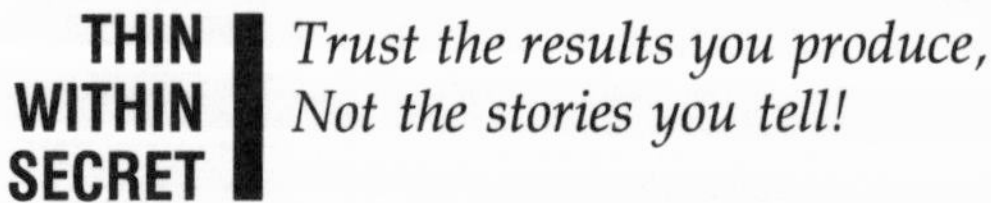

THIN WITHIN FOOD LOG

Hunger #	Time	Items	Amount

THIN WITHIN OBSERVATIONS AND CORRECTIONS CHART

Observations	Day 11
1. I ate when my body was hungry.	
2. I ate in a calm environment by reducing distractions.	
3. I ate when I was sitting.	
4. I ate when my body and mind were relaxed.	
5. I ate and drank only the things my body *loved.*	
6. I paid attention only to my food while eating.	
7. I ate slowly, savoring each bite.	
8. I stopped before my body was full.	

DAY 12

Will I Love Myself More?

One of the important goals of *Thin Within* is to inspire you to reclaim the power you've given away to food, the power that has been in the hands of your Fat Machinery. The key questions to ask yourself in order to stop your Fat Machinery are: "Am I hungry?" (this means are you at a 0, not sort of hungry, but empty), and, "Will I love myself more if I eat this?"

I've found, in working with thousands of people, that the greatest motivating force in weight mastery is not will power, as we may have thought in the past, but *love power*.

We all know how to love others. In fact, overweight people tend to say yes to everyone but themselves. Lisa Lowe, one of our graduates, tells how her mother taught her always to be *second* best. To do for others before she took care of herself, to sacrifice and compromise. She thought this was what you were supposed to do as a wife and mother. The problem is that when you are always nurturing others, sooner or later the well runs dry. The solution is to love, nurture, and support ourselves first so we have more than enough to give others.

OUR HEART SCALE

I visualize the heart as a deep well. Sometimes, although not very often, that well is replenished from the outside, from rains that are an incredible gift. But more often that well is replenished, enriched, and nourished by our own inner springs. And the question "Will I love myself more if I eat this?" is a powerful, self-nurturing tool for the heart if we answer it honestly and act accordingly.

This brings us to something that is just as dependable as our Hunger Scale messages but even closer to our core. That is, of course, our heart.

We can trust what our heart communicates to us. We can trust our intuition. We can trust that small inner voice that in answer to the question, "Will I love myself more?" says yes or no.

Believe your answer. Go with it as strongly and earnestly as you accept being at a 0 or not. What I've found for myself and for our graduates is that as you become conscious of your 0, you will become more conscious of your heart. Graduates tell me again and again that they always knew there was a positive flicker inside but that Thin Within really helped them ignite it into a flame. You can ignite this flame any time to nurture yourself. You yourself can replenish your well so that others can receive from and be nurtured by you. Once a month, for instance, Lisa now treats her body to a massage, and she always feels thinner and more loving afterward. We tend to feel thinner and then *become* thinner when we do loving, supportive things for ourselves.

OBSERVE AND CORRECT

"Will I love myself more?" is a good question to use as a loving way of observing and correcting ourselves. Perhaps you say yes to other people at times when actually it does not serve you. When you ask yourself this question, answer it immediately according to your heart's response. Your heart gives an accurate reflection about the truth of what you're experiencing at the moment. Pay attention—your heart can be trusted.

Adeline Rice says that "Thin Within is the glue that helped put my shattered life together." If Thin Within is the glue, then the question "Will I love myself more?" is the superglue. A little of it goes a long way.

Another pertinent question is, "Will I love myself more if I am with this person?" I have found that the presence of some people definitely enriches my life, while others seem to drain my energy.

During the time I gained weight after my abortion, I found myself associating increasingly with negative and less goal-directed people. During my period of positive growth and through the experience of developing Thin Within, the quality of my life improved along with the quality of my friends.

The question, "Will I love myself more if ______________?" will occur as often as you ask yourself if you're hungry. The Thin Within way of life is a melody that you are writing for yourself. And your answer to that question will let you know if you're in perfect tune!

GUIDING SIGNS

I have a little sign on my telephone that asks, "Will I love myself more if I say yes?" I have a tendency to overextend myself and make far more commitments than I can fulfill, and this is a gentle reminder and a way of learning every day to listen to my heart.

In the evening as I review my day, I ask myself two questions: "In what ways today did I clearly demonstrate my love for myself?" "In what ways today did I not demonstrate my love for myself?" By observing and putting in appropriate, compassionate corrections, the process of mastery becomes an incredibly self-nurturing, learning experience.

When I began working with people and their weight problems, I had only a vague awareness of the importance of the relationship between the inner spirit and the outer body. Sadly, I had seen many people, including myself, lose weight without losing their self-hatred. They become thin people with heavy heads and hearts, not realizing their own radiance.

The Thin Within tools will allow you to experience exciting internal as well as external changes as you love and nurture yourself down to your natural size. As the weight peels off so will each layer of self-hatred.

One of the greatest compliments I've ever received was from a man who stood up in a workshop and said that the reason he had come to Thin Within was not because he was overweight. He knew a woman in his church who had gone to Thin Within and been transformed from an ugly, negative person into a really loving woman who happened to become naturally thin. He had come to Thin Within because he wanted what she had.

That transformation is in large part based on the fact that love is the greatest of motivating forces. We'll continue to talk about this throughout the book, but for now make the question, "Will I love myself more . . . ?" the guiding question and the guiding light in your daily life. It will help you create the *body* and *life* that you deserve.

SUCCESS TOOLS

• Today ask yourself "Will I love myself more if I eat this?" Paste it on your refrigerator, in your wallet, by your desk, bed, car. It works!

• Continue to keep your Food Log and mark your Hunger Numbers.

• Continue to mark your Observations and Corrections Chart.

• Use the Thin Within Keys to Weight Mastery.

THIN WITHIN SECRET

One way of loving myself more
Is to create
A supportive environment
That nurtures me.

THIN WITHIN FOOD LOG

Hunger #	Time	Items	Amount

THIN WITHIN OBSERVATIONS AND CORRECTIONS CHART

Observations	Day 12
1. I ate when my body was hungry.	
2. I ate in a calm environment by reducing distractions.	
3. I ate when I was sitting.	
4. I ate when my body and mind were relaxed.	
5. I ate and drank only the things my body *loved*.	
6. I paid attention only to my food while eating.	
7. I ate slowly, savoring each bite.	
8. I stopped before my body was full.	

DAY 13

Present Time

You now have a choice to make. If you really want to stay the way you are, don't continue reading *Thin Within.* Quit right now. However, if you truly want to melt down to your natural size, then participate 100 percent in these exercises. Do them in succession, every day, using the Success Tools regularly, and you'll accomplish your weight goal easily. The more you use these tools the more natural they will become until eventually you will use the Thin Within Keys to Weight Mastery with little conscious effort. And you will enjoy eating so much more (or should I say less)!

Completing *Thin Within* will not *change* most of the circumstances of your life—you'll have the same spouse, the same relationships, the same boss, parents, kids, house. What will change with weight mastery is the skill to recognize and correct Fat Machinery behavior. You will be able to eat from 0 to 5 in all social settings and your behavior will be appropriate because it will be motivated by love for yourself. And that is why you'll melt down to your natural size and stay there.

THE PRESENT MOMENT

"There is simply the rose; it is perfect in every moment of its existence . . . But man postpones or remembers; he does not live in the present, but with reverted eye laments the past, or, heedless of the riches that surround him, stands on tiptoe to foresee the future. He cannot be happy and strong until he too lives with nature in the present, above time." (Ralph Waldo Emerson, "Self-Reliance")

When we were children we fully experienced present time, moment to moment. Do you remember squealing with delight at the simplest things? Nature also brings our focus into present time. It's very hard to have our heads in the past or future when we are caught in a sudden rain or snowstorm! But as we become adults, we often lose sight of where we are. If we find the moment difficult to deal with, we may wallow in the past or project into the future.

What a shame to look down at your empty plate and ask, "Who ate that? Where did it go?" Or to find yourself preoccupied with the past or future while missing out on the joy of making love. Some of us pass our entire lives in this way. It's as if the world were spinning by without our participation. Nothing is being experienced fully or completely!

If you use the Thin Within Keys to Weight Mastery, sit and eat slowly, and if you take the time to enjoy your food, knowing it's perfect in that moment, then you begin to be in present time.

Spencer Johnson, in his book, *The Precious Present*, says, "The richness of the present comes from its own source . . . When you have the present you'll be perfectly content to be where you are . . . It is the present that nourishes you."

HOW CAN I HAVE FUN DOING IT?

By all means don't deprive yourself while using the tools of *Thin Within*. When people come to me with problems, I often ask them, "How can you have fun dealing with this problem? How can you nourish yourself along the way? What kind of support would you like?" I want this experience of releasing all of your excess weight to be one that is utterly enjoyable.

When we were fat, we were always waiting until we got thin before doing things, whether it was to buy that leotard or new swimming suit, to take that dance class or vacation, or to risk the adventure of finding a new job or new place to live. We can spend a lifetime waiting to get thin.

I say, do it now! Eat 0 to 5 *now,* and you *are* a thin person. Start having fun while you wait for your body to catch up!

THAT LOVELY LITTLE RED DRESS

At Thin Within we have support groups for people after they have taken the workshop. I love to spend time with our graduates because I learn so much from them. It is most exciting and rewarding to see them actually doing what they've always wanted to do.

I was very touched by the experience of Jenny Statler, who had released 40 pounds. She had never been in a clothing shop that stocked clothes smaller than a size 16. She was so intimidated about shopping alone that one of the men in her support group, Ed, offered to take her.

Jenny said, "We were in the women's silk dress section at Macy's. Ed kept holding dresses up to me. 'I can just see you in that,' he'd say. 'Please,' I answered, 'people might hear you.' Then he found a red silk dress with diagonal stripes. He rubbed the silk on my arm and then held it up to me. I had been saying, 'No, no, no,' to every dress until I felt that silk on my arm and saw how stunning it looked. 'Wow,' I said, letting out my breath. I knew I wanted it but I couldn't let myself buy it. I felt too intimidated. The next night my support group convinced me *I really did deserve* to have that dress. When Ed called the next day offering to pick it up for me, I gleefully said yes. Today that lovely little red dress is in my possession!"

That's living in present time. Listening to that inner voice that says, "You deserve that stunning outfit—go for it!"

SUCCESS TOOLS

• Do something that you've always wanted to do, like Jenny. Go buy your equivalent of that "lovely little red dress." Don't put it off, do it today. Do something you've always wanted to do but have been afraid to do. Do something that you have avoided doing until you got thin. Get a manicure.

Buy flowers. Join an exercise class and wear a leotard. Go bicycling. Every time you are adventurous and take a risk you are strengthening that naturally thin person inside of you.

• Continue to use your Food Log and keep your Hunger Numbers.

• Continue to mark your Observations and Corrections Chart.

• Use the Thin Within Keys to Weight Mastery.

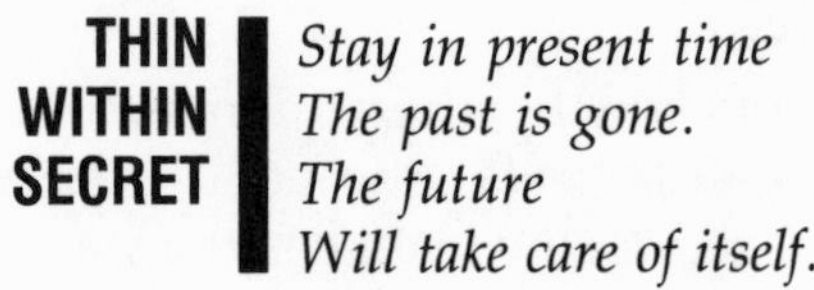

THIN WITHIN SECRET

Stay in present time
The past is gone.
The future
Will take care of itself.

THIN WITHIN FOOD LOG

Hunger #	Time	Items	Amount

THIN WITHIN OBSERVATIONS AND CORRECTIONS CHART

Observations	Day 13
1. I ate when my body was hungry.	
2. I ate in a calm environment by reducing distractions.	
3. I ate when I was sitting.	
4. I ate when my body and mind were relaxed.	
5. I ate and drank only the things my body *loved.*	
6. I paid attention only to my food while eating.	
7. I ate slowly, savoring each bite.	
8. I stopped before my body was full.	

DAY 14

The Perfect Chocolate-Chip Cookie

Thin Within gives you permission to eat the foods you love and permission to eat only the best. In the Thin Within process of weight mastery, nothing is "fattening," nothing is forbidden, nothing is "bad" for you.

It's interesting that when we listen to the messages of our body we find ourselves eating differently. Virginia Lottworth says, "I now listen and give my body what it wants. I find I love sweet-and-sour things, a baked potato with cheese and sour cream, sweet-and-sour pork. I love cheesecake. I think sweet-and-sour must be some kind of comment about my life."

Sometimes I have a craving for something soft. Other times it's protein or something crunchy—maybe a salad, nuts, or carrots. In the days ahead we'll be talking about healthful eating and how marvelously your body can balance your food intake (if you listen to it) so that you can be absolutely, fantastically healthy.

Before Thin Within I had lots of colds and many serious illnesses. This was at a time when I was fat and not listening to my body's messages. I frequently explained away my extra 38 pounds by saying how much I loved food. As I have used the Thin Within tools and have become attuned to my body in a loving way, I have found myself eating more fruits and vegetables, grains and natural foods, and less red meat. Since I grew up in a meat-and-potatoes family, at first my beliefs said one thing and my body said another. However, the more I listened to my body and joined in partnership with it, the more healthy and energetic I became. And I can now sincerely say that I love and appreciate food more than ever.

One of the most exciting results of the Thin Within way of life is when you discover your own unique program—the type and amount of foods your body loves best and that will produce a radiant and healthy, naturally slender you.

Today we'll talk about how to rate foods so that you will increase your eating pleasure. If you think you already love food, just wait!

There are three basic types of foods, and I don't mean fats, carbohydrates, and protein. They're called pleasers, teasers, and total rejects.

PLEASERS

Pleasers are those *very special* foods for which we have a particular affinity—foods that for us are 10s. Here are the characteristics of pleasers.

1. Our desire for a pleaser starts before we see or smell it.

2. We crave it or have a yearning for it deep down from inside. It is something that our bodies, not our heads, request, and it is so special that it gives total body satisfaction.

3. A pleaser may not be readily available. It might be a special dish at a particular restaurant on the other side of town, or the blueberry pie that only your mother can make. In other words, you would walk a mile to get it.

4. It's totally satisfying when you eat it.

5. It's very specific.

6. Pleasers change. It may take practice and patience to discover your true pleasers, but you can do it. You may have noticed thin people who eat unusual foods at unusual times. They are listening to their bodies (which experience only hunger, not time), and they are eating the pleasers their bodies want.

Three of my pleasers are Häagen-Dazs coffee ice cream, my father's lemon meringue pie, and a homemade cashew chicken salad with poppy seed dressing.

The pleaser concept extends to all areas of your life. You should surround yourself with as many of them as possible, for they are what makes life totally satisfying. Sometimes we must wait a long time for a certain pleaser. I would accept nothing less than a total pleaser in the man I was to marry, and I waited for forty-three years before I found him. I can tell you the wait was worth it! Accept only pleasers in your life and you will experience absolute satisfaction.

TEASERS

In an average home, 90 percent of the foods are teasers. Teasers are what we grab when we're not hungry and just want something—anything—to eat.

1. A teaser is convenient and easy to get.

2. Teasers generally are eaten when our Fat Machinery is in high gear.

3. Teasers look better than they taste.

4. Teasers are really not much more than stuffers and fillers, and we often overeat them for precisely that reason. They give our body no real satisfaction.

5. A teaser isn't on our minds until we hear about it, see it, or smell it. Part of the reason for being overweight is eating too much of what we don't really want!

6. Stop eating your pleasers when you reach that comfortable 5 or less, because the all-time classic teaser is what's left of your pleaser when you are satisfied.

There is another important difference between pleasers and teasers. When we wait until our body is truly hungry, it sends us clear messages as to what food it wants. This is usually something we really love (a true pleaser), and we tend to eat just enough because it is *so* satisfying. On the other hand, if we eat when we're not truly hungry (what I call grazing), we don't get clear messages from our bodies. We tend to eat teasers and end up being totally unsatisfied. We *think* the solution is to eat more in order to experience satisfaction when, in fact, the solution is simply to *wait* until we are hungry for the pleasers to call out to us!

TOTAL REJECTS

These are the foods not worth mentioning: too sweet, too salty, too fatty, artificially flavored, artificially colored, boring, unimaginative, don't-even-really-taste-good-yucky-foods with no redeeming qualities. Let's hurry on!

PLEASERS AND TEASERS EXERCISE

List some of the foods that are true pleasers for you. Be very specific.

____

____

____

____

List some of the teasers you have in your kitchen right now.

____

____

____

____

Get rid of those teasers! They stimulate your Fat Machinery and complicate your process of weight mastery. Remove the temptations so you have more room for pleasers—in all aspects of your life. Keep the pleasers! You deserve to have them! This is the beginning of a process of building trust with yourself around pleasers. You may want to start with small amounts, then, as you give yourself permission and build up your trust, you'll be able to have your pleasers sitting on your counter and you'll walk right on by if you're not hungry.

It's amazing how different our lives become if we choose whole body pleasers rather than the diet foods of the past. I used to "try" to lose weight by eating salads, grapefruit, hardboiled eggs, cabbage, and skinless chicken. Can you begin to see more clearly why diets don't work? They're made up almost entirely of teasers! Remember, too, the importance of the environment when you eat. Make the place you eat a pleaser as well!

If you go into a restaurant (you're at a 0) and your body says it wants a medium-rare filet mignon, don't settle for anything less. If it's not done to your satisfaction it's a teaser rather than pleaser. Speak up! Send it back! Ask for, and get, what you *really* want. You deserve to have it exactly the way you want it. If you're with a group who is settling for warmed-up frozen pizza and you know where to get a true pizza pleaser, go for it! You deserve the best.

SUCCESS TOOLS

• Rate your food as either pleasers or teasers in your Food Log. You can rate them from 0 (awful) to 10 (fabulous), or simply P or T.

• Tomorrow you will get to experience your very first all-pleaser meal. You'll be having a meal, preferably alone, consisting only of pleasers. You may go to a restaurant, fix it yourself, or have someone prepare it for you. Read over Day 15 and prepare for it.

• Examine and question all parts of your life, since you deserve pleasers everywhere. Is your home a teaser? Your car? Your job? Your relationship? How can you change a teaser into a pleaser?

- Continue using your Observations and Corrections Chart.
- Use the Thin Within Keys to Weight Mastery.

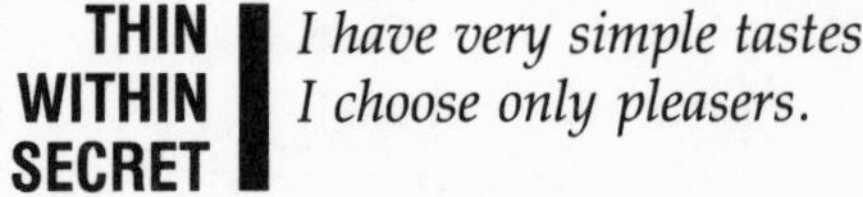

I have very simple tastes.
I choose only pleasers.

THIN WITHIN FOOD LOG

Hunger #	Time	Items	Amount

THIN WITHIN OBSERVATIONS AND CORRECTIONS CHART

Observations	Day 14
1. I ate when my body was hungry.	
2. I ate in a calm environment by reducing distractions.	
3. I ate when I was sitting.	
4. I ate when my body and mind were relaxed.	
5. I ate and drank only the things my body *loved*.	
6. I paid attention only to my food while eating.	
7. I ate slowly, savoring each bite.	
8. I stopped before my body was full.	

DAY 15

The Very First Meal of Your Life

Today you're going to have the privilege of eating a meal *totally* in present time. You're going to eat this meal as if you were a stranger in a strange foodland.

On Day 1 you answered questions about your last meal. You now have a sense of how you used to eat compared with the Thin Within way of eating. I call this exercise the Very First Meal of Your Life because you're going to slow down your eating in a very conscious way so you'll have an even clearer sense of how we eat at Thin Within. It's very important that you experience this meal when you're at a nice, healthy 0 so you can feel complete satisfaction and receive maximum benefits.

This meal is to be perfect, consisting only of pleasers. It can be one that you prepare for yourself or one that is served to you. In either case you are to pick your absolutely favorite spot in which to eat. The atmosphere is as important as the foods you choose, so surround yourself with things you love—your favorite china, silverware, crystal, lighting, music. If you eat in a restaurant, choose an ambiance that delights you. If you choose to have a picnic, select the perfect spot. It is best to eat this meal alone. However, you may have someone with you if that person totally supports you while doing this exercise.

This perfect meal is truly a gift you are giving yourself. You're going to make love to every single bite, so don't miss it!

When I did this exercise, I ate my perfect meal on a table set with a French linen cloth, silver, crystal, a Steuben vase with a red rose in it, and candles. (I love candlelit tables!) I ate in my favorite sitting area with a stunning view of the San Francisco Bay. I had my hair freshly done, wore an elegant white dress, and felt as if I were going to meet my true love. And I was—myself. I sat in this beautiful environment and savored every delicious bite. It was a perfect meal in a perfect spot, and I'll never forget it. May yours be as memorable as mine was!

Since you are to be the honored guest, treat yourself like royalty in preparation for your special feast. Pamper yourself with a massage, a vigorous workout, or whatever would be a treat for your body. Dress up. Have fun preparing for it, and, above all, enjoy the main event.

THE FIRST MEAL OF YOUR THIN LIFE EXERCISE

Read the instructions completely before starting, then proceed through the meal, slowly following each step.

1. Select your favorite spot and wear your favorite clothes.

2. Check your hunger level. Be sure you're at 0 so that you can truly enjoy the food.

3. When you sit down notice everything about the environment. No matter how familiar it may be, look at it as if you have never seen it before.

4. Before you start eating, become aware of every item of food. Notice how it looks on the plates. Smell it. Can you anticipate from the smell how it will taste? Before taking your first bite, you might want to repeat this little saying that I enjoy: This food I am about to eat will turn into health and beauty in my body. This food I am about to eat will support and sustain my naturally thin self. I thank You for it.

5. Before chewing the food move it around in your mouth.

Notice how you experience different flavors as you put the food in different parts of your mouth.

6. Bite it. What kind of a sound does it make? Chew it slowly. When you swallow, notice the aftertaste.

7. Sample each item and then ask yourself if it was a pleaser or a teaser. Is it *really* a pleaser for you? Or did you just think it was? Remember that what formerly was a pleaser may not be now. Pleasers can change.

8. After tasting every item on your plate ask yourself if this is really a 10 meal. How would you rate each item on a scale from 0 to 10?

9. Before you continue eating, check in with your Hunger Numbers. Where are you on the Hunger Scale? Stop eating when you're a comfortable 5. Remember, your empty stomach is only as large as your *fist*.

10. When you've finished eating, spend some time enjoying yourself and savoring your experience. Write down your feelings and observations about the meal.

Observations About My Perfect Meal

___

___

___

___

___

___

___

___

___

___

___

This is how we eat at Thin Within. We eat only pleasers. We chew our food slowly, smelling it, tasting it, luxuriating in it. Enjoy your food in this fashion. Bask in it. Thin Within gives you the wonderful opportunity of making love to your food. And in making love to your food, you're making love to yourself. As we eat only the very best foods in this manner we will create our most radiant, healthy bodies.

SUCCESS TOOLS

• Continue keeping your Food Log, marking your Hunger Numbers, and rating your foods as pleasers or teasers.

• Continue marking the Observations and Corrections Chart.

• Use the Thin Within Keys to Weight Mastery.

THIN WITHIN SECRET

Until Thin Within
You haven't begun to taste
The pleasers
In your life.

THIN WITHIN FOOD LOG

Hunger #	Time	Items	Amount

THIN WITHIN OBSERVATIONS AND CORRECTIONS CHART

Observations	Day 15
1. I ate when my body was hungry.	
2. I ate in a calm environment by reducing distractions.	
3. I ate when I was sitting.	
4. I ate when my body and mind were relaxed.	
5. I ate and drank only the things my body *loved*.	
6. I paid attention only to my food while eating.	
7. I ate slowly, savoring each bite.	
8. I stopped before my body was full.	

DAY 16

The Power in Simplicity

At Thin Within we believe there is great power in simplicity. By that we don't mean simplification, but, rather, a kind of simple rightness that flows. There is no greater power than telling the whole truth on a moment-to-moment basis. I would like you to use this power of truth today by establishing an honorable relationship with me about you and *Thin Within*.

Tell me something. Have you been sitting in the stands crunching on your munchies, reading *Thin Within* but not really using the Success Tools? In other words, have you been watching the weight-loss game rather than participating in it? Let's be frank. Today is Day 16. You have, including today, just 15 days to reach the weight-loss goal you set for yourself.

Before we continue with what I consider the most exciting part of *Thin Within*, stop a minute and look at your progress so far. Have you scrambled out of the stands and gotten down there on the field and participated 100 percent? That means doing the *Thin Within* exercises daily and incorporating the Success Tools into your daily life. If so, then miracles are beginning to happen in your life. And even more exciting adventures are in store for you in the second part of this book, as we proceed from how we have constructed our Fat Machinery to how we can invent our own personal Thin Machinery.

But first, pause for a moment. Take a few deep breaths

and close your eyes. Tell yourself the whole truth. On a scale from 0 to 100, how much have you participated so far? Write it down in the space below. Remember, the truth will free you!

I, ________________________, have participated ____ percent so far in this *Thin Within* book.

As Thin Within graduate John Herrick likes to say: "Until Thin Within, I never told the whole truth—I ate it instead!" If your participation so far is less than 100 percent, be kind to yourself and simply make a correction that will help you create an environment in which you can generate the desired results.

Whenever I think of participation, I think of Toby Bartholomew, who came to Thin Within as if she had been shot out of a cannon. She was so excited because she had discovered that one of her very overweight relatives had become a model for Eileen Ford after taking Thin Within. Toby dropped four dress sizes while taking the workshop and the rest of her 70 pounds came off effortlessly in the following few months.

On the other hand, one of my workshop leaders, Martha Swanson, resisted the entire time she took the Thin Within workshop. "From the beginning I liked what I heard, but I felt I couldn't do it. At that time our kitchen was being remodeled. We had no stove or refrigerator and had to eat out all the time. My daughter and I couldn't figure out how we could follow the Thin Within Keys to Weight Mastery without a kitchen. I blamed my lack of participation on other people and circumstances. I was not taking responsibility. Second, I was lying to myself. I used only 30 percent of the Success Tools, and I didn't follow the Thin Within Keys to Weight Mastery. I thought being a participator meant talking about it, which I did. I told everyone how it didn't work." But Martha continued to participate in the Thin Within process and released over 40 pounds, which she has kept off for six years.

So don't chastise yourself. Use the Observations and Corrections Chart with compassion as you put in corrections at the places where you aren't participating. You don't have to go back and redo all your Success Tools. However, you do need to allow yourself to hit 0 and eat to 5 or less, and to use the Thin Within Keys to Weight Mastery. Ask yourself, "Will I love myself more if I let go of all the weight I deserve, using the Thin Within process?" Your answer will tell you exactly what you need to know in order to proceed effortlessly and from the heart.

YOUR DREAMS ARE YOUR RACE CAR

Some people have cars that are mere tools for them, just a means of transportation. But for me a car is a work of art, and I love it to be fine-tuned so it purrs as I travel from place to place.

That's how I like to think of Thin Within—that we show you how to do it so thoroughly that you actually purr yourself to your weight goal is if in a Porsche.

One of the ways we rev up for our last 15 days is to commit ourselves to the following:

I, ______________________, now choose in present time to commit myself to be a ____% participator or spectator.

When we talk about commitment we mean that profound alliance to oneself and one's personal goals. It's not to Thin Within. Nor is it the usual negative idea—I should commit myself, I must do this. In fact, Day 16 is a good time to ask yourself if you are really committed to this process. Be honest with yourself. Are you reading this as if it were a novel instead of participating in it as a workbook? If the commitment to yourself to *do* this process and melt down to your naturally slim self is not there, then put down this book and come back to it when you have the inner desire *to go for it for yourself!* That's what commitment is: "I am going to do it 100 percent for myself and no one else. Therefore, I am willing to press myself, to do it differently, and be unreasonable all along the way."

REFOCUS ON YOUR GOALS

Now, refocus on your three basic goals, remembering that your first goal is the amount of weight loss you want to achieve and your other two goals are about anything that will support your naturally thin self.

So with your eyes closed touch your stomach and abdomen and ask your body how many pounds you have released so far. How many do you still want to let go?

DAY 16 GOALS

Today's date:________________

Present weight:________________

Desired weight:________________

Now restate your three goals (or choose new ones) in a positive, result-oriented manner.

Goal 1 I will weigh ____________ pounds by Day 30.

Goal 2 I will ________________________ by Day 30.

Goal 3 I will ________________________ by Day 30.

HITTING ZERO

Eating only when you hit 0 is the kind of simplicity I was talking about at the beginning of this day. Before discussing how to have your life be exactly the way you want it, let's be certain you know how to tell when you're really at 0.

I once had a naturally thin friend who used to say to me, "You know, Judy, you never let yourself get hungry before you eat." I stared dumfoundedly at him. I had no idea what he was talking about. Hunger? Are you kidding? I didn't eat because I was hungry. I ate totally out of Fat Machinery—because I was bored or lonely or sad. I ate to please my friends or my mother. I ate when I heard certain songs on the radio or recalled certain memories. I ate preventively because I didn't think I would get enough to eat. My favorite was tourist eating, which meant if I didn't have that crab gumbo tonight, I was afraid I might never have another chance to eat it again.

I remember when I was a child and I'd come in from playing, absolutely famished. And I remember what the food tasted like at those times. The first bite was like heaven. Tasting heaven is what hitting 0 is like. It's a deep-down wonderful feeling of lightness. And, when you're there, everything tastes—what can I say, magical.

At first this process of hitting 0 may feel somewhat unfamiliar to you. This makes sense because you are in a new land. But don't worry. We've given you a map for that land. Just wait until you're at 0, then eat anything your body wants, and stop at 5 or less. If you will allow yourself to go through this unfamiliar territory, you will quickly find that it becomes home for you and you will look forward to being hungry before you eat.

You have probably noticed already that your body doesn't require the amount of food that you used to eat. Indeed, it feels good to eat less. That's why the visualization of your stomach being the size of your fist is so powerful.

Remember that, at Thin Within we don't believe in "kinda hungry" or "a little bit hungry." You're either at 0 or you're not; 0 means you are truly hungry and you can eat, and "not" means you're not hungry so why eat?

Don't ask your head about hunger. Instead, use the Bodometer Process—close your eyes and touch your stomach and abdomen and ask, "Am I at 0?" and then ask, "What would my body love to eat at the present moment?"

"I'M HAVING A LITTLE TROUBLE HITTING 0"

I can't tell you how long it will take for you to get to 0. It varies with each person.

In one workshop I told everyone to wait until they hit 0 before they ate. The next week a rather heavyset man raised his hand. "Well, Judy," he said, "I was having a little trouble hitting zero. I just didn't know whether I was hungry or not."

"Oh," I said. "Well, when did you last eat?"

"Hmmm," he said, scratching his head. "Well, you said

to wait until 0. I guess . . ." he looked up, "seven days."

"Seven days ago?"

"Yeah," he nodded. "You said not to eat until we knew we hit 0 and I haven't been hungry for seven days."

Now there was a man who participated 100 percent!

I'm not recommending that you should wait seven days to eat. However, do wait until your body hits an unequivocal 0. As I said, I can't tell you how long it will take before you get truly hungry. Thin Within does not advocate fasting, strict denial, or harshly imposed discipline. But trust your body and know that realigning yourself with your natural rhythms of hunger and comfort is very healthy for you.

So be gentle with yourself and listen to your Hunger Numbers. Let your body tell you the whole truth.

THE HUNGER GRAPH

One of the most effective tools to help you become familiar with your hunger level patterns is the Hunger Graph.

I'm convinced that a good tool is transparent. This means that after using it for a while you don't even notice it. Remember when you were a child and learning to use a pencil was so difficult? Then fairly quickly you didn't even notice how effortlessly you were using it? This will happen for you with the Hunger Graph.

By the end of *Thin Within* you won't need the graph anymore because you, yourself, will have become the perfect tool. You'll just naturally wait until you feel hungry before eating and, at a certain point, you'll stop because you've had just enough.

The Hunger Graph is another way to help you become conscious of these Hunger Numbers. It will not replace your Food Log. The way to use the graph is to record the time you eat and your Hunger Numbers before and after eating. The example shows how the graph would look if you were at a 1 when you ate at 11 A.M. and were at a 6 when you finished. Then by 5 P.M., you had drifted down to a 0 and ate to a 5. And at midnight you ate from a 2 to a 5. So each time you eat or drink during the twenty-four-hour period you record the time and the before and after Hunger Numbers.

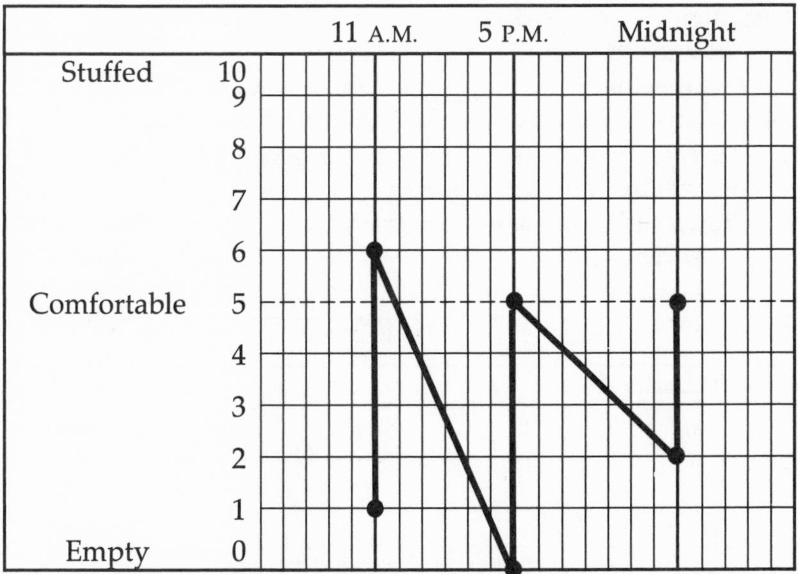

The Hunger Graph is an excellent technique to demonstrate the kinds of eating patterns that develop throughout your day. Suppose when you check your seven Hunger Graphs at the end of the week you see that at your daily 11 A.M. coffee break you tend to start eating when you're not at a 0 and you go above a 5. Why? What is in your environment that is stimulating your Fat Machinery? Maybe you eat because your friends asked you to go on a break, not because you are hungry. Consequently there's a real danger (because you didn't start at a 0) of eating above a 5. You may also be talking while you eat and not being conscious of the Thin Within Keys to Weight Mastery. So observe the patterns from your Hunger Graph and put in the corrections. Look for creative options. Maybe you'll wait and eat by yourself after the break (if you are hungry) so you can be more conscious of your eating. Maybe you'll choose not to eat at midnight (see the graph) so you'll truly be at a 0 the next morning, and you may even choose to "hold" until 11 A.M.

We give you the Hunger Graph first because it's an excellent visualization of your eating patterns, and, secondly, it ties your Hunger Numbers to time. This allows you, as in the example above, to see the patterns that aren't working for you and then to put in the correction. When you identify your problem areas, the question to ask is, "What is going on at those times that is not supporting me to eat like a thin person?" And, lastly, this graph is an excellent way for you to see when you're eating because of true body hunger and when you're eating because of Fat Machinery.

Take a look at the graph again.

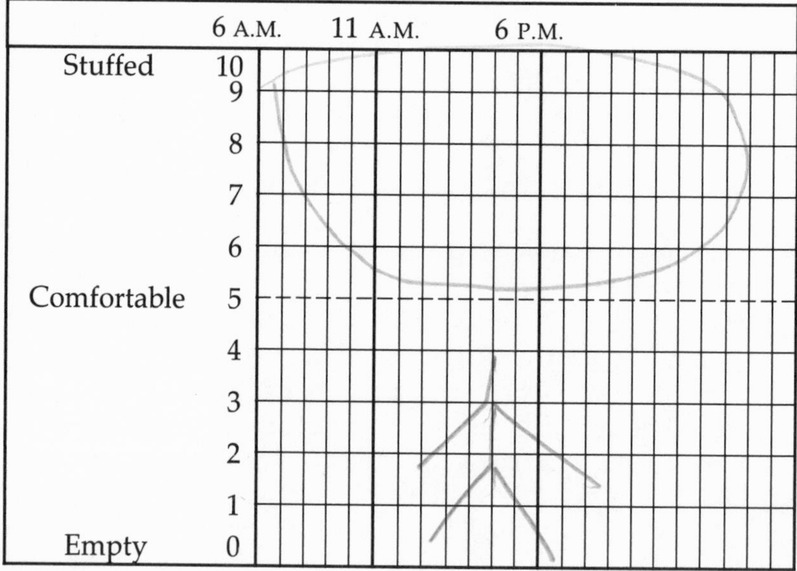

Extend the dotted line at 5 to the right. Draw a big circle above the line. Now draw a stick figure below the line. If you eat above 5, you're fueling that Fat Head or doing what we call psychological eating. If you're eating 0 to 5, you're creating that naturally thin body by doing what we call physiological eating—feeding the body.

This is another example of the power behind telling the whole truth about your body, emotions, and environment, and how all these have an impact on your eating patterns. The quicker you identify the unworkable patterns and put in the corrections, the easier you'll get to your weight goal.

RIDING YOUR 0

One of the ways to speed up your weight-loss process and make your Hunger Numbers more accurate is to go through the process of riding your 0. When I ride my 0 it simply means that I sometimes choose not to eat even though I'm at a healthy 0!

Suppose on Friday I eat about 1 P.M. when I'm at a 0. The next time I'm hungry it may be about 8 P.M. (this changes every day, of course) and I may choose not to eat. I deliberately commit myself to ride my 0 and may wait until noon or later the next day before I eat. In other words, I choose to skip a meal when I'm at 0 in the evening and 0 the next morning. It really is all right not to eat even though your body may be hungry.

This is a very effective way to speed up your process and to help you have a clearer sense of where your 0 is and what it feels like at various stages.

BULIMIA AND ANOREXIA NERVOSA

One of the reasons that Thin Within has been so successful with people with bulimia and anorexia nervosa is that when you eat 0 to 5 and not 0 to 10, you stay beneath the point that triggers the compulsive behavior of binging and vomiting. Diana Lewin came to Thin Within suicidal and totally immersed in the purge-binge syndrome. As she said, "I was eating to a 10 when I came into Thin Within. I was even eating out of the garbage."

Another thing that we've discovered about bulimia and anorexia is that both conditions are based on low self-esteem with the underlying belief of "I don't deserve." What happens with compulsive overeating is that it becomes an incredibly vicious circle. Eating over a 10 lowers your self-esteem, which in turn strengthens your "I don't deserve" belief, and this perpetuates the compulsive overeating.

For a bulimic to learn to stop at a 5 is the beginning of a natural reversal of the process, because eating above a 5 is what triggers the compulsive vomiting.

And, of course, for an anorectic, listening to your body and giving yourself permission to go ahead and eat until you're comfortable is an enormous step. It is one made out of love and trust, with the sure knowledge that you will not gain excessive weight if you eat to a comfortable 5 or less.

SUCCESS TOOLS

• Fill in your Hunger Graph today, marking in your hunger levels and connecting the lines so you can observe your eating patterns. You might want to copy this graph out of the book and carry it with you at all times so you can be sure all your numbers are accurate. Remember, too, that if you mark down one number (say, a 5) and twenty minutes later you feel like you've eaten to a 7, then go back and correct your numbers—because the last reading you get is the accurate one!

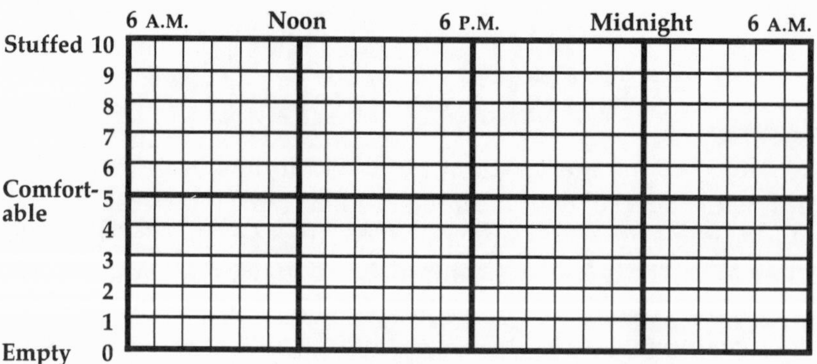

• Continue to keep the Observations and Corrections Chart.

• Use the Thin Within Keys to Weight Mastery.

THIN WITHIN SECRET

There's a power in simplicity.
In 0 to 5 eating
Less becomes more.
And when we pay attention
To every detail
We come closer to perfection!

THIN WITHIN OBSERVATIONS AND CORRECTIONS CHART

Observations	Day 16
1. I ate when my body was hungry.	
2. I ate in a calm environment by reducing distractions.	
3. I ate when I was sitting.	
4. I ate when my body and mind were relaxed.	
5. I ate and drank only the things my body *loved*.	
6. I paid attention only to my food while eating.	
7. I ate slowly, savoring each bite.	
8. I stopped before my body was full.	

DAY 17

An Eagle Among Eagles

One of my best friends was a girl named Paula. We ate the same foods—mostly candy, hamburgers, french fries, and malteds. Paula never gained weight and I got fatter and fatter. I couldn't understand it. I knew she had some magic I didn't have. We had the same life-styles and we did the same exercises in gym class, yet she stayed thin and I got fat. I thought that either her body had to be special or she had some secret. I even asked my mother. We decided that Paula was one of the lucky ones—her metabolism was faster than mine.

If only I had asked Paula a few questions about her eating habits and listened to her answers, I would have learned the secret for myself. And I could have created for myself the same success as Paula.

You can find the same magic. You can discover the same secret. This is what Day 17 is all about. But first I want to go back to Day 8 and highlight a part of the eagle story that is very important here.

Do you remember when the naturalist took the eagle up to the mountain and tried to *push* him into flying? What happened? The eagle wouldn't budge. He just kept looking down at the chickens. After all, the chickens were all he knew. Of course he chose to be a chicken.

The naturalist, on the other hand, looked at the eagle and saw him as clearly as if he were on a TV monitor. He observed him and longed to put in the simple correction that would set him free.

But the eagle wouldn't budge.

All of us see others more clearly than we see ourselves. We see that untapped potential just waiting to be freed. But instead of allowing others to put in the correction for themselves we try to do it for them. And the problem, of course, is that people are reluctant to accept any correction but their own.

That's why this book is vital to your weight-loss process. We know you have to put in your own individual corrections. You believe only when you see it for yourself!

What happened to the eagle was that he was alone on the mountain without a comparison. He saw the sky and he saw the chickens. What the chickens were doing looked pretty good to him. They were safe. They had more than enough food and they were his pals. He didn't have a comparison that would allow him to see it could be different. It was only when the naturalist put the eagle in an environment where he could see other eagles that he had the opportunity to make a comparison between chickens and eagles.

That's exactly what we're going to do today. We're going to look at the behavior of naturally thin people. If you look only at the behavior of people immersed in Fat Machinery, you'll have no comparison, you'll have no possibility of making the transition from fat to thin.

Think of that eagle when he sees the other eagles for the first time. He is awestruck and his heart begins to beat rapidly. He sees them flexing their wings in the sun, then gliding off the mountaintop and swooping and diving. And he feels their power and dignity and he wants what they have.

So what does he do? He doesn't need the naturalist anymore. He presses himself. He just *acts as if* he were an eagle and flies off the rock. And lo and behold, he discovers he was an eagle among chickens all along.

LISTENING TO THE BEHAVIOR OF THIN PEOPLE EXERCISE

Think for a moment of a friend or a person you have known who is naturally thin. Not dieting thin, not can-eat-only-diet-foods thin, a-life-full-of-deprivation thin, but naturally thin. Someone who does not need to diet. Someone who eats anything he or she wants to eat, someone who is thin from within. Look at his or her life and pick out those things you notice that seem to contribute to making them naturally thin.

Don't take a long time; just jot down what you remember about how he or she acts.

The Behavior of My Naturally Thin Friend

____

____

____

____

____

____

____

____

____

____

____

____

____

____

Besides my friend Paula, I recall my friend John who has always been pencil-thin. My friends and I used to think he was weird because of his eating habits. He would eat only when he felt like it, and when he did he ate only a little bit. I remember once we had a delicious chocolate fudge layer cake and he ate only the frosting. We made fun of him, but he didn't care. He just ate what he loved to eat and left the rest behind. He also had a lot of stamina and energy. He wasn't as interested in food as we were. Instead of meeting us at a restaurant, he'd rather go to an art museum, a park, or a movie. He was a doer.

Does my friend John sound familiar to you? Yes, in his own unique way he was following the Keys to Weight Mastery. He ate only when he was hungry and then just enough (a mere fistful) to satisfy his body. He ate slowly and paid attention to the food. When he wanted to talk, he talked, and when he wanted to eat, he ate. John is just one example of a naturally thin person. Joy and I studied many, and found that they all practiced some of the eight Keys to Weight Mastery.

THIN PEOPLE LIVE IN THE FAST LANE

Do you see how you're already on your way to being a naturally thin person?

You're not waiting in line to be thin—you're already there! You leave food on your plate. You eat what you love and in the combinations that please your body. Food is just one of many enjoyable pleasures in life. As you are releasing your excess weight, you're also releasing a lot of bound-up energy that can be used to enjoy more fully your family, work, and play.

Isn't life great? As one of our participants said, "Thin people live in the fast lane."

Diane Schmidt, who took Thin Within when she was sixteen and slipped from a size 12 to a size 4, now, six years later, is a wardrobe consultant for men. Diane said, "I tell my men, 'If you weigh more than you want, it's because you're eating more than your body needs.' You see a naturally thin person eating an ice-cream cone and you say, 'Oh, poor me, I couldn't do that. I'm so unblessed. They're lucky. They have a better metabolism than I.' But that may not be true. That ice-cream cone may be all that naturally thin person had to eat all day. What is true is that naturally thin people *tend* to eat less."

That's it. That's what we do in Thin Within. We point out

the tools that help you eat less. From now on you will begin to eat less until it becomes a natural rhythm. You learn to dance with it: waiting until 0 takes you as partner and stops twirling you when you're at a 5 or less.

And what is exciting about Day 17 is that today you have just solved the mystery for yourself—*being* naturally thin is *behaving* naturally thin using Thin Within's eight Keys to Weight Mastery.

No matter what your metabolism, genetic structure, or body type, you can weigh exactly what you want to weigh and stay at that ideal weight forever. That's weight mastery. And you discovered the secret in the exercise you just completed. You have drawn a picture of what a naturally thin person *does*. They eat until they're comfortable. They take risks. They're apt to be more interested in living and loving than in eating. When they eat, they eat. When they read, they read. When they talk, they talk. They don't mix it all up. They remain conscious. Sometimes they eat the frosting instead of the cake. Sometimes they eat cake instead of dinner. Sometimes they have beans for breakfast. They don't follow convention. They don't eat for anybody except themselves. They love their bodies and listen to them. Thin people aren't induced or seduced by food. They share. Sometimes they choose to have an appetizer instead of the five-course dinner everyone else is having. And you know what? Afterward, they want to dance instead of snooze.

So, whenever you're in doubt about what to do as a naturally thin person, turn back to today and look at what your eagle among chickens looks like.

In any situation, all you have to do is ask yourself, what would a naturally thin person do?

So, that's the secret. If only I'd known at twenty-one that my friend Paula was thinner than I because she ate less, I would have saved myself a lot of anguish. But then I didn't have Thin Within to tell me how to eat less in a way that would make me really want to do it. That's the real secret.

You're no longer stuck with the chickens, comfortably pecking endlessly away because of their Fat Machinery. You're in the fast lane now, my friend, riding with the naturally thin ones.

SUCCESS TOOLS

• We learn by questioning and listening to the eagles in our lives. Watch the naturally thin people around you. They will support you in this treasure hunt to find your Thin Self. Whenever you meet one, ask them directions.

• Fill in your Hunger Graph, marking your hunger levels and connecting the lines so you can observe your hunger patterns. Lines have been added for you to list all food and drink you've consumed today so that as you record your hunger levels you are also keeping a Food Log. Does this seem like a lot of work? You will very quickly internalize all of this. For now, keeping a day-to-day Hunger Graph and Food Log is a way of learning to eat consciously.

• Continue keeping the Observations and Corrections Chart.

• Follow the Thin Within Keys to Weight Mastery.

THIN WITHIN SECRET

When faced with a problem,
Ask:
What would a thin person
Do right now?

HUNGER GRAPH

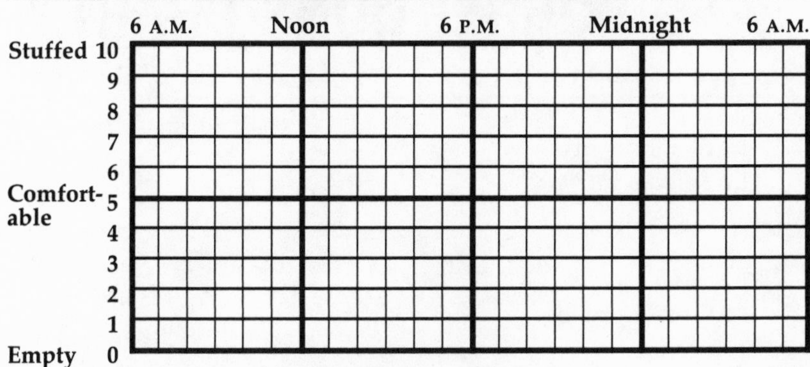

FOOD LOG

Enter all food and drink for 24 hours.	Time

THIN WITHIN OBSERVATIONS AND CORRECTIONS CHART

Observations	Day 17
1. I ate when my body was hungry.	
2. I ate in a calm environment by reducing distractions.	
3. I ate when I was sitting.	
4. I ate when my body and mind were relaxed.	
5. I ate and drank only the things my body *loved*.	
6. I paid attention only to my food while eating.	
7. I ate slowly, savoring each bite.	
8. I stopped before my body was full.	

DAY 18

Going with the Flow

I love to dance. I can't remember a time when I wasn't moving to music in some way. My heart's desire was to become a dancer. But when I asked my parents if I could take dancing lessons, they said no. They felt dancing was frivolous and impractical as a career. However, I never stopped wanting to dance. I went to every musical and every Fred Astaire movie. I adored Gene Kelly and pretended I was Ginger Rogers or Cyd Charisse. And, alone behind closed doors, I'd dance in my bedroom until I had the steps just right. I fell asleep at night watching myself on the stage. But I followed my parents' advice, pursuing more realistic careers in dental hygiene and nursing until I was twenty-nine. At that point I felt that if I didn't start dancing then, I never would. I knew I'd feel unfulfilled forever if I didn't go after my dream.

Looking back, it seems a bit presumptuous as a twenty-nine-year-old novice to have interviewed only the best dance companies in the Bay Area, but I firmly believed that not only would I take classes, but that I would be invited to join a first-rate company! In fact, I was so excited and optimistic after I chose the Shawl-Anderson Modern Dance Company, that I told the head instructor, Luisa, that within two years I'd be an active member of the company. She smiled politely and patted me on the shoulder. I had no idea until years later that every aspiring student said exactly the same thing!

Yet, looking back, I know now something *was* different. I

was absolutely, totally dedicated to fulfilling my dreams. In Thin Within terms we would say I practiced 150 percent! I danced morning, noon, and night, practicing as a registered nurse in between pliés and relevés. I loved every single moment of it. I knew I was a dancer and I knew that this was my last chance. And, after a year and a half, six months ahead of schedule, I was invited to become a member of the company! The interesting thing is that my technical ability did not compare with those who had started dancing as children or young adults. So why me? How did I fulfill my dream? I may not have been the most skilled technically, but I believe the reason I succeeded is because I had heart.

MILES AND MILES OF HEART

Heart means to me that compelling belief felt deep inside that convinces us from the tips of our toes to the hair on our scalps that we deserve to have absolutely whatever our heart desires. It is the vision of exactly what we want to create in our lives and how much of our life spirit we will invest to achieve those dreams.

When I danced my way into that company I had no idea what process I was following. I now know that what I was doing was going with the flow of my universe. You see, our universe flows in the direction of our deep-seated beliefs. If we believe that we are unworthy, then our universe will flow in the direction of unworthiness. As talked about in Day 8, if we believe we are chickens, even though we are eagles, then our lives will be lived as chickens. René Descartes said it beautifully: "I think, therefore I am." The flow of the universe starts with our deep-seated beliefs, which push us to do the actions that support our beliefs. This creates the results that corroborate our beliefs.

We naturally flow from

Belief ————→ *Action* ————→ *Result*

In other words, I *believed* I was a dancer (before I had proof or facts to subtantiate that belief), so I naturally did all the *actions* that made me a dancer. And, after a year and a half, I finally had the *results*—a reputation as an esteemed member of a first-rate dance company.

I flowed from

I am a dancer *(Belief)*	⟶	Practicing 100 percent *(Action)*	⟶	Member of dance company *(Result)*

Even though I was working very hard as a nurse and a dancer, it actually felt effortless, as if I were flowing downstream with the current of a river. This is because my actions were completely in alignment with my beliefs. Have you ever had this experience? This experience of going with the flow of my universe only became clear to me years later, when I examined another period of my life—one of great difficulty—when I clearly was going against the flow.

GOING AGAINST THE FLOW

Let me explain. My parents wanted my sister and me to become dental hygienists. This was fine for my sister, who believed it was the right choice for her and loved doing it, but it didn't make my toes tap. I wanted to dance, not clean teeth! Consequently, I did just enough to get by in dental school. Eventually I fell in love with a medical student, got pregnant, and quit school before graduating. I didn't accomplish the *result* of receiving a dental hygiene degree, even though I did the *actions*, because I *never believed* in it or wanted it in my heart. I found everything about it to be a constant struggle, from the biochemistry to working on cadavers. This is a good example of what happens when we "try" to accomplish a result by simply acting without the conviction or belief behind it.

THE BELIEF PROCESS

The difference between the dancing experience, where I was truly flowing with my universe, and the hygienist experience, where I was attempting to go against the flow, resulted from the fact that in the latter situation the essential core belief was missing. The natural flow, the one that works, is as follows:

STEP #1 *(Belief)* ⟶ STEP #2 *(Action)* ⟶ STEP #3 *(Result)*

Most of us tend to skip Step 1 and concentrate all our efforts on Step #2 and #3, the action and result stages. Why? Because in our culture we tend to be doers and havers rather than believers. We very rarely start with a core belief when we begin to do something. And problems often arise because, like my trying to become a dental hygienist, we're doing someone else's good idea for us and not our own.

STEP #1	⟶	STEP #2	⟶	STEP #3
No core belief; lacks conviction		Action therefore ineffective		Creates an incomplete or undesirable result

A perfect example of this is the naturalist whose good idea it was for the eagle to know he was an eagle. But the eagle had to discover this for himself. The naturalist could not force his beliefs on the eagle. The eagle had to learn to change his own beliefs.

GOING AGAINST THE FLOW IN WEIGHT LOSS

How this applies to weight loss is really quite simple. When we're overweight (or think we're overweight) we have a bedrock *belief* that we're fat. A 1984 *Glamour* survey corroborated this fact. Out of thirty-three thousand readers they found that no matter how thin women get, most still believe they're too fat. An overwhelming majority, 75 percent, said they felt "too fat" even though only 25 percent were actually overweight, according to standard height-weight tables. Furthermore, 45 percent of the women who were actually underweight still said they felt too fat and needed to go on a diet! These statistics sadly demonstrate what happens when we adopt external standards into our belief system—we often lose sight of what really is appropriate for our own unique bodies. The greatness of Thin Within is that it is a process of redirecting our focus back to the only true source—the wisdom of our own bodies.

All of us have a very strong core belief about our bodies. This belief is the first step in the process. Think for a moment what that basic belief is for you. For me (when I was carrying 38 extra pounds) it was that *I was fat!* (Step #1) And, because I believed I was fat (which I believed even when I weighed 125 pounds), I would act (Step #2) as people do when their core belief is that they're fat. Guess what that action was. Yes, *I ate too much!*

STEP #1	→	STEP #2	→	STEP #3
I am fat		Eat too much		Fat Body
(*Belief*)		(*Action*)		(*Result*)

The result of this behavior was absolutely predictable—*I had a fat body!* It all flowed smoothly because of my belief. However, the result was definitely not what I wanted!

Another action taken by people who have the core belief of I-am-fat is that of going on a diet—eating skinless chicken, cottage cheese, and grapefruit. The problem here is that we may produce the *result* temporarily of a thin body, but because we haven't changed our *core belief* (I am fat), we have what we call at Thin Within a Fat Head. Having a Fat Head is the opposite of thinking as a naturally thin person. It means living in fear of the fat person popping out at any moment, viewing all foods as fattening, counting calories, etc. This is exactly what the *Glamour* survey pointed out, and it is also the moral of the chicken-eagle story. If you believe yourself to be fat, you will accept this and live as a fat person, perhaps never experiencing the naturally thin person you truly are. People with Fat Heads feel as though they are masquerading in a thin body. How many times have you gone on an expensive, exhausting diet, reached your desired weight, and kept your fat clothes around . . . just in case? Getting thin in this manner is full of effort and struggle because you get caught up in a vicious circle that looks like this:

STEP #1	→	STEP #2	effort ↗ struggle ↘ → ↙ effort ↖ struggle	STEP #3
I am fat (*Belief*)		Diet and sacrifice (*Action*)		Fat head, thin body (*Result*)

Isn't this how we used to get thin for a vacation, party, or class reunion?

Do you know that in this country there are twenty-four thousand diets? This means you can change your actions twenty-four thousand times and still be fat. But all you have to do is change your belief *once* and you will achieve slimness effortlessly and forever! If you want lasting results (and I know you do!) then you must first go back to Step #1 and change your core belief from *I am fat* to *I am thin*. And I'm not talking about after you get thin! I mean right now, weighing exactly what you weigh, whether you're 5 or 105 pounds from your ideal size.

When we change our core belief (Step #1) from *I am fat* to *I am thin,* the actions that follow are the same as those of naturally thin people regarding food and eating. Thin people eat only when hungry and only those foods they love. And what is the result? That's right—a thin body *and* a thin head. And this is the reason they stay thin forever.

STEP #1	→	STEP #2	→	STEP #3
I am thin (*Belief*)		I eat 0 to 5 the foods I love (*Action*)		Thin body and thin head (*Result*)

WHY THIN WITHIN WORKS

This is what makes Thin Within unique and so successful. We know that the core belief that works is: *I am Thin Within.* This belief is the seed from which your naturally thin person will blossom. The root of weight problems and therefore your starting focus is at Step #1, your basic beliefs. The next four days will show you ways to go back to that seed—the core belief—and see what you have planted. Then I'll give you the tools to replant the seed so that you release your weight effortlessly forever. It is from this point on that a new Thin Within way of life begins. Just as I became a dancer effortlessly because I believed I was a dancer and have maintained my desired weight for more than ten years because I believe I am thin, so will you. This new core belief will remove the struggle, pain, and misery from releasing excess weight.

HOW TO CHANGE BELIEFS

The next four tools you'll receive will change the I-am-fat belief to the I-am-thin one and the I-don't-deserve to I-do-deserve-to-be-thin. These tools will allow you to plant new seeds within yourself.

First we'll start with Forgivenesses. This may sound like an odd place for a weight-loss process to begin, but believe me, from my experience with thousands of Thin Within graduates, you'll see that it is *exactly* where to begin. Our overweight bodies are a reflection of our resentments, guilt feelings, and unforgiven feelings. In order to release the excess weight we must first release those resentments and guilt feelings. For instance, you may have always resented your brother because your father favored him. Or, perhaps years ago you did something and still feel guilty about it. Start by forgiving your father, then your brother, and most importantly of all, forgive yourself for what happened.

After we do Forgivenesses we'll do Affirmations, Visualizations, and Daily Acknowledgments. These four tools will totally unravel that ball of yarn that has been your weight problem. They will facilitate your growth from the root level of a belief to a wonderful flowering maturation that will be permanent.

Because you are changing at the level of belief, the actions you will take (0 to 5 eating, the Keys to Weight Mastery, and other naturally thin behavior) will produce the desired results of your naturally slim self! It will look like this:

STEP #1	→	STEP #2	→	STEP #3
I am thin (*Belief*)		I use the Keys to Weight Mastery and Thin Behavior List (Day 17) (*Action*)		Naturally thin body (*Results*)

Created by:

- Forgivenesses—Day 19
- Affirmations—Day 20
- Visualizations—Day 21
- Daily Acknowledgments—Day 23

What we have talked about today is really the basis of Thin Within—that is, becoming naturally thin is a way of flowing with your universe from Belief to Action to Result.

Another way to look at this is: If you want things in your life to flow effortlessly, always return to Step #1, the heart of the matter, your spiritual center. If you begin at the center, at the level of your deep-seated *beliefs*, the natural flow is to the *mental* level and then to the *physical*, where you will realize the tangible results you desire:

Step #1	→	Step #2	→	Step #3
Spiritual		*Mental*		*Physical*

The main focus of *Thin Within* is to create a balance among the spiritual, mental, and physical aspects of ourselves. Diets, on the other hand, omit the spiritual aspect entirely, beginning only with Step #2, the mental. This creates, as was shown earlier, a vicious circle between the mental and physical (Steps #2 and #3), without producing the desired results. However, when we flow from a genuine belief, we achieve the result we truly desire with joy and ease. *And it will be permanent!*

BELIEFS THAT ARE SLOWING YOU DOWN

Before we start changing beliefs, let's examine some beliefs about thin people that might already be slowing you down. Jot down very quickly, in the space provided, any feelings, perceptions, or beliefs you have about thin people, including those that are both *positive* and *negative.*

My Perceptions, Beliefs, and Feelings About Thin People

____

____

____

____

____

____

____

____

____

____

____

____

____

____

Some examples that have been given in our workshops are: too vain, active social life, happier, more competitive, sickly, can't cook, don't really enjoy food, too picky, sexually promiscuous, more attractive, less attractive, less fun. . . .

Now circle all of the negative ideas or beliefs you recorded. Have you listed any negative beliefs significant enough to keep you fat? Ask yourself this question: "Is it any wonder that I'm not a thin person if I have so many negative beliefs about thin people?" Now cross out all of the negative ideas or beliefs you recorded.

Look at the positive ideas you have about thin people. Would having or being all of the things you recorded be so much that it might scare you? Would it be too good to be true?

Are there so many positive ideas that you don't think you could possibly live up to all of them? Do you *really* feel that you deserve to have all of that? Please be honest with yourself and answer these questions truthfully. Remember that you can have your life any way you want it to be. You choose to become what you want to be by choosing the beliefs you hold in your mind. Tomorrow, on Day 19, we will start by strengthening your ideas about how you really *do* deserve it all. On Day 20 you'll see how to affirm your beliefs in such a positive way that miracles will occur in all areas of your life.

SUCCESS TOOLS

• One of the things I experienced when I danced was the joy of moving, not from technique, but from within—the thrill of letting go, forgetting form, and letting the spirit within be the motivating force. In 1975, I taught a class called My Body, My Friend, which was about moving the body in a joyous, loving, and unencumbered way. This is what you can start doing today. Ask your body what kind of movement it feels like doing for fifteen minutes. Go at the pace your body wants. Let it speak to you. Ask it what activity it would thoroughly enjoy. Take a leisurely or invigorating walk, move to music, jog, bike, jump on a trampoline, swim. Do whatever your body wants to do as long as it involves movement. At Thin Within we exercise only for the joy of it, not for the weight of it. We move our bodies because we love movement, not because we want to lose weight.

• Fill in Hunger Graph today, indicating the weight you have released.

• Mark your Observations and Corrections Chart.

• Use the Thin Within Keys to Weight Mastery.

THIN WITHIN SECRET

Stay in present time
Change those beliefs
And go with the flow
Of your naturally thin self.

THIN WITHIN OBSERVATIONS AND CORRECTIONS CHART

Observations	Day 18
1. I ate when my body was hungry.	
2. I ate in a calm environment by reducing distractions.	
3. I ate when I was sitting.	
4. I ate when my body and mind were relaxed.	
5. I ate and drank only the things my body *loved*.	
6. I paid attention only to my food while eating.	
7. I ate slowly, savoring each bite.	
8. I stopped before my body was full.	

HUNGER GRAPH

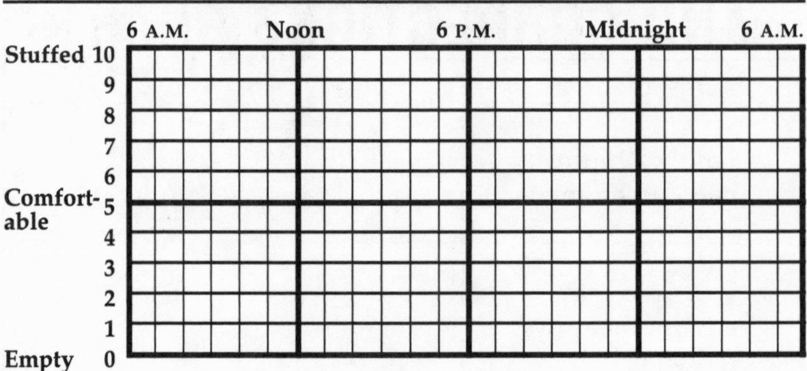

FOOD LOG

Enter all food and drink for 24 hours.	Time

DAY 19

Forgiveness: The Master Eraser

Many people come to Thin Within totally immersed in the anguish of Fat Machinery—a past that they believe cannot be repaired and a present that cannot be accepted.

Forgiveness in Thin Within is a way to complete the past. It is not used in a religious sense—for our sins. Nor is it used in the everyday sense, as a mother forgives a child for misbehaving. Rather, Forgiveness in Thin Within is a form of release. It is self-cleansing. If you don't forgive others, you will not forgive yourself and have room for all the good things you deserve, one of which is to have a body that pleases you. We realize that the word *forgiveness* may be a "loaded" one. For some, it may represent an invasion of privacy. They don't want to touch it. Also, they may believe that they have nothing in their lives to forgive. However, all of us hold on to our petty resentments, from being angry at the person who cuts in front of us on the freeway to hating the scale because it doesn't read the way we want it to (my friend in Day 6 could have saved a broken toe if she had used Forgivenesses instead of kicking it!). For others, forgiveness brings up a lot of fear. They ask, "If I forgive someone am I approving of the horrible thing they did to me? And does forgiveness mean I have to be friends with them?" Forgiveness does not mean that you condone what someone did. Nor does it mean that you have to have an ongoing relationship with that person. It is a letting go, a releasing of the resentment and guilt. If you can come up with a better word than forgiveness, then by all means use it. Call it the Master Eraser or Ajax or your Self-Cleansing Tool. But use it. Forgiving yourself and others releases you from the past so you can get on with your joyful new Thin Within life in present time.

You may ask "What if I don't feel like forgiving? Will it work?" And it's true that some of our workshop participants have believed that they must have a genuine feeling in their hearts before Forgivenesses work. However, the point of forgiveness is not in the realm of feelings. It truly is like cleaning out a house. If you want quality in your life, such cleaning must be done. It is an act of *intention.* We're not discounting your very real feelings here; they are valid whatever they are. But don't let your feelings block the powerful results that forgiveness produces.

STAYING STUCK

Let me also point out that a lack of forgiveness is a fantastic way of staying stuck in the past and closing off our future. It's also a great way to torture other people and perpetuate their guilt feelings. A lack of forgiveness blocks receiving. How can we allow ourselves to receive the blessings of a radiantly slim body if we've blocked the way with hatred and resentments. When we give up our anger and our desire for revenge, we set ourselves free!

Because Thin Within is based on cybernetic principles, we believe that our bodies are a moment-to-moment reflection of the state of our spirits. We believe that overweight results from retained or repressed resentments (a lack of forgiveness for others) and guilt (a lack of forgiveness for ourselves).

We also believe that as we forgive we release energy as well as excess weight. As this energy becomes available we experience a light-heartedness, a surge of creativity, and a renewed love for humankind. As one of our graduates, Sandra, says about these tools: "At fifty-one I can reshape my life. There's just something about getting in touch with the Thin Within adventure of going inside to lose weight. It's like a wonderful tunnel—a tunnel of self-discovery where you get to right past wrongs. You get to rewrite the movie saying to the little girl, 'But you silly little goose, it wasn't like that. You only thought it was,' and then you get to rewrite the entire script with Forgivenesses, Affirmations, and Daily Acknowledgments."

One woman in our workshop had always been very resentful at how her parents had pushed food on her when she visited them. During the workshop she talked about it and did Forgivenesses. When she went home for a holiday she noticed the strangest thing. They *didn't* push food on her. It was her perception about it, and doing Forgivenesses cleared her perception so she could see the truth.

We cannot change the past, but through forgiveness we can change our *interpretation* of it.

In Thin Within we believe that forgiveness is release. We believe that the fat on our bodies accumulates because of a combination of swallowed anger, retained resentments, and repressed guilt. And in order fully to release our weight we need to release our hatreds, resentments, and guilt. This means to let go with a sweet goodbye and gracefully step into the present moment with a renewed spirit.

So each day, from now on, pick one person for whom you feel some emotional charge (on that particular day), and write Forgivenesses about them that you will repeat ten times.

MY FATHER AND FORGIVENESS

Now, I'll be honest with you. When I started doing these Forgivenesses I did *not* like them. And I resisted them for the longest time! I thought they were silly, and the redundancy of writing the line ten times reminded me of when I was in fifth grade and had to write one hundred times that I wouldn't talk in class. But I made myself write the Forgivenesses. "I, Judy, forgive ______________________ for ______________."

And I'll tell you something. Today I am absolutely sold on Forgivenesses. And I'll tell you why—they work! An example from my own life is as follows: I didn't get married until I was forty-four. As you know, I let go of my 38 pounds; but I still was having relationships that were less than the perfect ones I genuinely thought I deserved. They were absolutely wonderful men but not the ones for me. I never could make that final commitment. Something didn't feel quite right.

Then a few years ago I realized that for thirty years I had been holding on to an incredible amount of unresolved resentment toward my father. He's an absolutely fantastic man and has always been very loving toward me. However, I resented the fact that he wasn't a business tycoon. Instead he owned and managed butcher shops. I know now that I had never forgiven him for not turning out the way *I* thought he should. And what I discovered is that my childhood resentments were definitely acting as barriers in my relationships with men.

So I used Forgivenesses regarding my father. I wrote: "I, Judy, forgive you, Dad, for not being the business tycoon I wanted you to be." And I wrote this and other Forgivenesses about my expectations toward myself and my father off and on for two years until I felt complete.

How did I know when the process was complete? By the results, which are your teacher. You see, clearing up the old resentments regarding my father had nothing whatsoever to do with him. It was *my* problem, since I was attempting to force my standards on him. Until my relationship with him was resolved I unconsciously felt that I didn't deserve to have a completely wonderful relationship with *any* man. I continued the Forgivenesses until I experienced nothing but unconditional love for my father. I knew then for the first time in my life that I was deserving of the best. Nine months later I met Arthur, who is now my husband, a perfect 10 for me.

MIRACLES

If you continue Forgivenesses as a lifetime tool, miracles will happen for you. If you're willing to release all your hatred and anger, resentment and guilt, including those that seem insignificant, the universe will totally support you. If you can let go of the past and allow yourself to be in present time, you will find yourself surrounded with grace.

When you catch yourself eating out of Fat Machinery, forgive yourself immediately. Don't harbor any resentment against yourself. You have suffered enough. Just forgive yourself, forgive others, and open yourself to the miracle of the moment—which means all that you have to do to get back on course is to wait until you hit 0 again.

When you find yourself on a plateau and you're not releasing the weight you'd like to, observe yourself as if you were on that TV monitor, searching for any places where you still hold on to resentment, anger, and guilt. Go back to Days 8, 9, 10, and 11, and be sure you've forgiven yourself. Then you'll start releasing the weight again easily.

Our bodies are reflections of our unforgiven resentments. All those things we don't forgive and don't speak out about (but eat over) are reflected in our shape. This is the weight of failure. This is the pain of holding on to the past. Open your hand, forgive, clean the slate, and let the radiance of a sparkling, naturally thin you emerge. You deserve it!

FORGIVENESSES

To begin I'd like you to turn back to Day 9, which was about how you created your Fat Story. Remember how you picked out four situations that really had an influence on your weight and eating? With each situation there is a list of the people involved. In the space below, list all the people for whom you hold resentments about your weight, food, or eating.

My Forgiveness List

____

____

____

____

____

____

____

____

____

____

____

____

____

____

Now, pick three of these people from whom you get an emotional charge today. Go ahead and systematically forgive each one, ten times.

Person #1

I, ________, forgive ________ for ____________.

1. ______________________________
2. ______________________________
3. ______________________________
4. ______________________________
5. ______________________________
6. ______________________________
7. ______________________________
8. ______________________________
9. ______________________________
10. ______________________________

Person #2

I, ________, forgive ________ for ____________.

1. ______________________________

2. ______________________________
3. ______________________________
4. ______________________________
5. ______________________________
6. ______________________________
7. ______________________________
8. ______________________________
9. ______________________________
10. ______________________________

Person #3

I, ________, forgive ________ for ____________.

1. ______________________________
2. ______________________________
3. ______________________________
4. ______________________________
5. ______________________________
6. ______________________________
7. ______________________________
8. ______________________________
9. ______________________________
10. ______________________________

Did you feel like getting up and going to the refrigerator as you did this exercise? Or perhaps you feel some release or even exhilaration? Do you see how our resentments, anger, and guilt can stimulate Fat Machinery? If you have any observations about yourself in relationship to these three forgiveness exercises, write them down in the space provided. This is a good way to give yourself feedback.

My Observations About the Forgiveness Tool

FORGIVENESS AND OUR GRADUATES

I recognize that writing Forgivenesses may seem unfamiliar at first. I'm not asking you to believe *me* that they produce dramatic results in one's life but to *find out for yourself.* If you find that you get along better with your mate, your boss, your family, your children, or your coworkers, then you will know from your own experience that it is a powerful tool for you.

One of our graduates wrote Forgivenesses about her brother during the workshop. She was totally estranged from him, didn't even know where he was, and had not spoken to him in twelve years. She wrote her Forgivenesses about him for seven days until she felt the process was complete. The next morning she got a phone call from Australia. It was her brother.

SUCCESS TOOLS

• Write your Forgivenesses daily. Choose someone for whom you currently have a negative emotional response and write an appropriate forgiveness, such as "I, __________, forgive my mother for forcing me to clean my plate."

• Don't forget to write forgiveness statements about yourself and your participation in your fat story. "I, __________, forgive myself for abusing my body with food."

• When you're suddenly irritated with yourself or someone in your life do a verbal forgiveness on the spot. Remember our overweight is stuck resentment and guilt. And every little forgiveness counts.

• Continue to fill in your Hunger Graph.

• Continue to keep the Observations and Corrections Chart.

• Use the Thin Within Keys to Weight Mastery.

THIN WITHIN SECRET

I breathe in my naturally thin self,
I breathe out resentments and guilt.
I breathe in forgiveness,
and breathe out excess weight.

HUNGER GRAPH

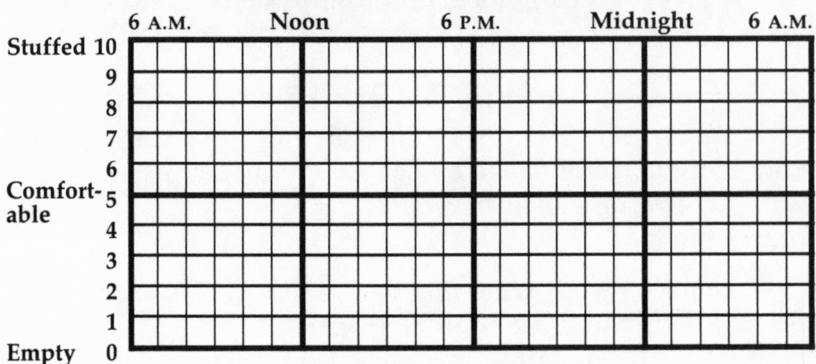

FOOD LOG

Enter all food and drink for 24 hours.	Time

THIN WITHIN OBSERVATIONS AND CORRECTIONS CHART

Observations	Day 19
1. I ate when my body was hungry.	
2. I ate in a calm environment by reducing distractions.	
3. I ate when I was sitting.	
4. I ate when my body and mind were relaxed.	
5. I ate and drank only the things my body *loved*.	
6. I paid attention only to my food while eating.	
7. I ate slowly, savoring each bite.	
8. I stopped before my body was full.	

DAY 20

Affirmations: The Golden Nugget

Once there was a poor man walking sadly along a road, and a very rich man came up to him and handed him a golden nugget. The rich man told him that the nugget would make him very rich. The poor man went home and, indeed, become very rich. A few years later as he was walking along the road, he saw a poor man and gave him the nugget. This poor man immediately rushed off and had the nugget appraised. And do you know what he discovered? The nugget was only painted brass.

He remained a poor man.

The moral of this story is that he who believes himself to be rich is rich.

This story is a wonderful illustration of how an affirmation works, and it also demonstrates the Thin Within principle of Belief ⟶ Action ⟶ Result.

An affirmation is like a golden nugget that you plant in the fertile soil of your mind, and out of it springs all that you desire.

Human beings are cybernetic processes which can be programmed either positively or negatively. This means that we direct our reality through our thoughts. Forgivenesses and

Affirmations are a way to move from negative, unworkable thoughts to positive, creative ones.

The theory of affirmations goes back to the work of Emile Coué, a renowned French psychotherapist who cured many of his patients with the following technique. He had them repeat, 20 times, 3 times a day: "Every day, in every way, I am getting better and better." This was based on the principle that our subconscious mind can hold only one thought at a time and that it will always accept the stronger of two thoughts. Therefore, if you constantly repeat positive affirmations they will prevail over negative thoughts. Whether or not you agree with the theory, find out for yourself. *Affirmations work!*

APPLYING AFFIRMATIONS TO WEIGHT LOSS

I, Alicia Smiley, am a naturally thin person. I do what thin people do, and I weigh 120 (enter your desired weight) pounds.

The above affirmation goes with the flow of workable beliefs explained on Day 18.

It starts with a *BELIEF* (I am naturally thin) and flows to an *ACTION* (0 to 5 eating, using the Thin Within Keys to Weight Mastery, doing what thin people do) and produces a wonderful *RESULT* (your desired weight).

Note also that it is written in the present tense. This is because an affirmation is concerned with changing what exists *right now.* You may question saying, "I, Sarah, am 155 pounds right now," because it's not true since, at this moment, you actually weigh 200 pounds. The reason we write Affirmations as if they are real, in the present moment, is that in order to bring our dreams into reality we need to create the context for them *right now.*

This incredibly powerful approach to weight mastery has helped thousands melt down to their naturally slender shape, and it can do the same for you. We actually program our minds and direct our own reality by language. And while this programming may be done by thinking or speaking, the most powerful way is with repetitive writing.

FORGIVENESSES AND AFFIRMATIONS

In Thin Within we always combine Forgivenesses and Affirmations. When we forgive we move out of the past into present time. We are cleaning the slate. This is why forgiveness is often called the Master Eraser. When you do Affirmations you are writing a request on that clean slate. This changes the I-don't-deserve-to-be-thin to I-do-deserve-to-be-thin!

The fundamental principle is that we direct our reality through our thoughts. By following Forgivenesses with Affirmations we are releasing negative Fat Machinery and replacing it with new, positive, Thin Machinery.

LISTENING TO YOUR RESPONSE

While you are writing the above affirmation, pause a moment and listen to how your mind is responding. It will tell you what is stopping you from having what your heart desires. Thank your mind for sharing. Forgive yourself and create another affirmation (if need be) to clear it; then go back and continue writing the original affirmation.

For instance, let's say you're busy writing this Affirmation, "I, Judy, am a naturally thin person and I do what thin people do and I weigh 114 pounds." Okay. Now pause and listen to your mind's response, which may be, "Oh, no you're not. You're not even close and furthermore you don't deserve to be because you might be so attractive that you'll go out and have an affair." You might think that if you let go of all your excess weight you'd be too attractive and perhaps become promiscuous. This is a good example of how a belief can limit our growth.

To clear away these obstacles use the Forgiveness and Affirmation Tools. First forgive yourself for your fears. "I, Judy, forgive myself for being afraid to wait until 0." Then create a positive affirmation to follow. For instance, "I, Judy, deserve to be physically attractive, naturally thin, and weigh 114 pounds." Or you may say, "I, Judy, deserve to be my stunning, naturally slender self and be totally committed to my marriage."

It's very important that you feel totally safe as you melt down to your naturally slender self. I understand how often we cushion and protect ourselves with fat on the outside because we feel small and afraid on the inside (more about this on Day 23).

The beauty of the Affirmation Tool is that we can take our own trembling hand and learn to love ourselves into courage.

What you're actually doing as you write and listen to your mind's response is releasing the old, unworkable beliefs that have produced nothing but negative results. You now have an opportunity to replace them with new, positive Affirmations which will support you in reaching your realistic weight goals!

AFFIRMATIONS AND YOUR FAMILY

There are so many incredible stories in Thin Within about the value of Forgivenesses and Affirmations that I cannot begin to recount them. However, I do want to share with you one of the most touching stories about the power and effective application of Affirmations.

One of our Thin Within workshop leaders has a ten-year-old daughter, Katie, who was two years behind the rest of her class in school. This was most disturbing and was breaking her mother's heart. Katie felt stupid and ugly and thought there was no hope since she was such a slow learner. And everyone else at school believed it also. Her mother had visited the school countless times, talked to teachers, helped Katie with her schoolwork, and nothing seemed to work. So one day she decided that as a last resort she would use the Thin Within Affirmation Tool.

Every night before Katie went to sleep her mother asked her to say 10 times: "I, Katie, am smart." Then 10 times: "I, Katie, am beautiful." Then 10 times: "I, Katie, learn easily."

In the morning her mother asked her to repeat the same three Affirmations 10 times. Within three months Katie caught up with *two years* of school! This story demonstrates how, when we change our beliefs, our actions will flow into perfect results. Katie's teacher now uses the technique of Affirmations in her classroom!

When you hit a plateau or whenever you feel stuck, ask yourself whom you still haven't forgiven; forgive them 10 times. Then write the following affirmation 10 times: I, ____________________, am naturally thin and no longer afraid of feeling terrific!

WILLINGNESS AND PATIENCE

It's very important in this process to be *willing*. Sometimes before we can have what we really want, we need to ask ourselves if we are willing to have it. A good affirmation for this is: "I, ____________________, am willing to melt down to my natural size and have it all."

Another point I'd like to make is the importance of being *patient* during this process. These ideas may be new to you, so give your mind a chance to consider and to accept them. You may have had the belief for years that you're fat, that you'll always be fat, that you don't deserve to be thin. So as you're being gentle and loving with your body, also be that way with your mind. Simply do your Forgivenesses and your Affirmations and see what happens.

Florence Pinco, one of our graduates who totally changed her life after she took the workshop, applies Forgivenesses and Affirmations to all areas of her life. "I use Forgivenesses and Affirmations throughout my day, in my work, and for my own personal guidance. On the way to work I say, 'I deserve to be successful today. I deserve to be successful with my clients and to be accepted by my colleagues.' At my old job there was one woman who was a real pain in the neck. I knew I could not really be in present time in my new job until I forgave her. And that's exactly what I did. I now have my absolutely dream job. This is because the concept of 'I deserve' has become my watchword. I said to the man who interviewed me, 'This job is mine.' And all during the interview I was thinking, 'I deserve to be liked by this man.' I was and got the job. Now I'm working on forgiving my husband for not being a romantic!"

"THAT'S FOR ME!"

Have fun doing your Affirmations. Record them on tape with a musical background. Write or listen to them in the morning as you're getting up and at night as you're falling asleep. Play them in your car on the way to work or while you're doing something with your hands that doesn't require thought, like working in the garage or washing the dishes. You can say them to yourself in front of the mirror or to a friend.

Mary, one of our graduates, said to me in a support group meeting, "I'm taking my body out to play this weekend and every time I see a beautiful body on the beach I'm going to say the following affirmation: 'That's for me!' "

SUCCESS TOOLS

• Write Forgivenesses in which you forgive yourself for your role in creating your own food, eating, or weight problem. Write it 10 times a day: I, ______________________, forgive myself for ______________.

____

____

____

____

____

____

____

____

____

____

• Follow it by today's affirmation written 10 times:

I, ______________________, am now a naturally thin person (Belief) and I do what thin people do (Action) and weigh ____ pounds (Result).

____

____

____

____

____

____

____

• Continue to mark your Hunger Graph.

• Continue to mark your Observations and Corrections Chart.

• Use the Thin Within Keys to Weight Mastery.

THIN WITHIN SECRET

The most powerful way
To manifest anything
In your life
Is through Forgivenesses and Affirmations.

HUNGER GRAPH

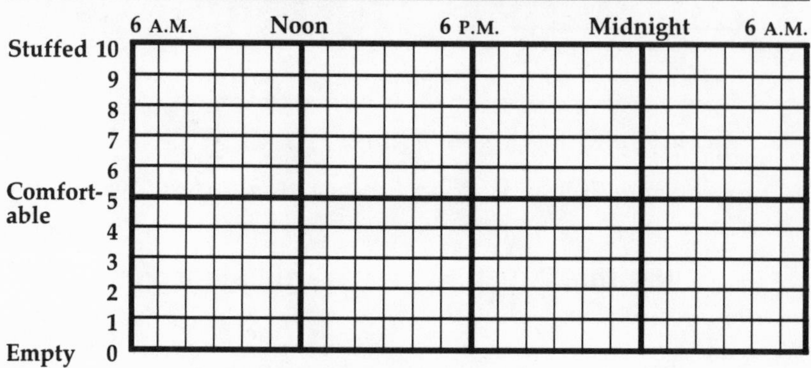

FOOD LOG

Enter all food and drink for 24 hours.	Time

THIN WITHIN OBSERVATIONS AND CORRECTIONS CHART

Observations	Day 20
1. I ate when my body was hungry.	
2. I ate in a calm environment by reducing distractions.	
3. I ate when I was sitting.	
4. I ate when my body and mind were relaxed.	
5. I ate and drank only the things my body *loved*.	
6. I paid attention only to my food while eating.	
7. I ate slowly, savoring each bite.	
8. I stopped before my body was full.	

DAY 21

A Living Vision

There has been a lot written in *Thin Within* about your naturally thin self. We now know that we all have one within. Today let's go back and reunite with your Thin Self in a special way so that it becomes a living vision within you.

While you do this exercise, play your favorite music, something that is peaceful and soothing.

BREAKING THROUGH MY WALL OF FAT

Get into a comfortable position. Take a deep breath and relax as you exhale. Good. Take another deep breath and relax. Now read these instructions very carefully and close your eyes as much as possible as you do the imagining (Taping this exercise, then playing it back with your eyes closed, is very helpful.) Slow down and really take time to see it all. Then when you have a clear sense of it (you may *feel* it more than *see* it), open your eyes and record your experience.

Remember, the more you slow down and really think about it, the more insight you'll have. And also remember there is no correct answer—whatever comes to mind or whatever you see or feel is correct for you.

Okay. In a few moments you're going to close your eyes and imagine that you are at the movies, and that the movie, in full Cinemascope and Technicolor, stars you as your naturally thin self in a beautiful rolling meadow.

Now take a deep breath, relax as you exhale, read these instructions and then close your eyes. You will open them after a few moments, write down your feelings, read some more instructions, and, while breathing deeply, close your eyes again.

Okay, now see yourself on that screen as a thin person, looking exactly the way you want to look, feeling exactly the way you want to feel, out in this beautiful, open rolling space. . . .

This is a very unusual movie because at any time you can extend your hands and create your Thin Self. You can shape your body lovingly as though you were a sculptor, for in this process you can have it exactly the way you want it.

Go ahead and do it . . . no one is here except you and me, and I'm behind you 100 percent. Go for it!

Is there a face to your body? Don't forget the backside . . . don't leave out any details. Good. Now stand back from your Thin Self and make sure you are exactly the way you want to be. Add any last-minute touches. Fine.

Now see yourself on that movie screen as this thin person, doing things, moving about, dancing on those rolling green hills with the blue sky sparkling above . . . feel the wonderful ease in which you live and move. . . . See someone joining you in the dance. How wonderfully you move together. Don't you feel great? Your body truly supports your purpose in this life. . . . It feels so good, you feel ecstatic!

How I See Myself and How I Feel As My Naturally Thin Self

____

____

____

____

____

____

____

____

Now imagine that you are going to create a wall of food and fat around this glorious thin person that you truly are. . . . Extend your hands out in front of you and start building that wall of food and fat. . . . Put it all in there. . . . You might have a few people stuck in your wall. . . . Some unexpressed emotions . . . some beliefs. . . . As the wall gets higher and higher it's okay to feel that sense of desperation and frustration . . . you can't even see your Thin Self, can you? The wall has totally concealed you from your Thin Self. . . . Stand back and take a look at your wall of food and fat. . . . Describe what you have put in it. . . . Are there people in your wall? How big is it? How solid? What does it feel like? Does it smell? Notice any feelings that you have about your wall right now and write them all down.

My Wall of Fat

Okay. Imagine that your wall of food and fat can talk to you. . . . Let it speak.

What do you want to say to me, Wall?

____

____

____

____

Now imagine that you can say exactly what you want to that wall of food and fat. . . . Go ahead and say it.

Well, I have a few things to say to you. . . .

____

____

____

____

Now, thank your wall of food and fat for the great job it's done. It's been a buffer, an excuse for not doing things, and in some ways a real buddy. Your wall has served you well. . . . Thank it for all it's done and make sure it hears you.

Now, you are just about to destroy your wall of food and fat. . . . Pause a moment and notice any last-minute considerations. Now tell the wall of food and fat that you're going to demolish it and listen for its answer. . . .

Now, when you're ready, destroy your wall of food and fat. Extend your hands out in front of you and actually knock it down. Get rid of that wall! Destroy every last bit of it any way you choose. . . . Good.

And, now that the wall is destroyed, what do you see? What is on the other side of your wall? Is that you? Are you that light, radiant, wonderful, naturally slender person standing there so gracefully? Free at last? Write down what you see and how you feel.

Reuniting with My Thin Self

VISUALIZATIONS IN YOUR DAILY LIFE

The process you just experienced is called visualization. It can be done mentally or can be written or drawn. It is the process of taking your affirmation—I am a naturally thin person—and forming a whole picture with it. It is the experience of a *feeling*-thought. It is the visual form of your affirmation.

When I was a little girl I used to visualize myself dancing for hundreds of people. It was so real to me that I could actually hear their applause and I could feel the sweat gleaming on my skin. It was like a feeling insight. Years later when I actually danced in a modern dance company, what inspired me to dance morning, noon, and night was this same vision which I never lost. No matter how exhausted I was or how discouraged I became, I was able to continue dancing because of the power of this internal image.

Your visualization of your naturally thin self can be just as powerful for you. As one of our graduates Ralph Pintora says, "My visualization was a very precious gift. It was an experience of the potential within myself. It is understated physical power balanced by a profound tenderness and compassion. I often recall that vision. I've never lost it. It is definitely I and who I am in the process of becoming."

SUCCESS TOOLS

• See what forgiveness is appropriate for you today. Turn back to Day 19 and pick someone from your Fat Story (or pick someone in present time) whom you need to forgive and write the Forgiveness 10 times.

___

___

___

___

___

___

___

___

___

___

• Affirmations, 10 times today:

I, ____________________, deserve to be a thin person and ______________. For instance, "I, Judy, deserve to be a thin person and take a trip around the world." Choose something that is meaningful to you and that you really want. Use the same affirmation all day. This combination of Forgivenesses followed by Affirmations is very powerful and produces results. However, be sure you choose something you really want and are willing to have—because you're going to get it!

- Continue to mark the Hunger Graph.
- Continue to fill in the Observation and Corrections Chart.
- Use the Thin Within Keys to Weight Mastery.

THIN WITHIN SECRET

What I can visualize
I can actualize.
I do deserve to have it all—
A naturally thin body,
A perfect life!

HUNGER GRAPH

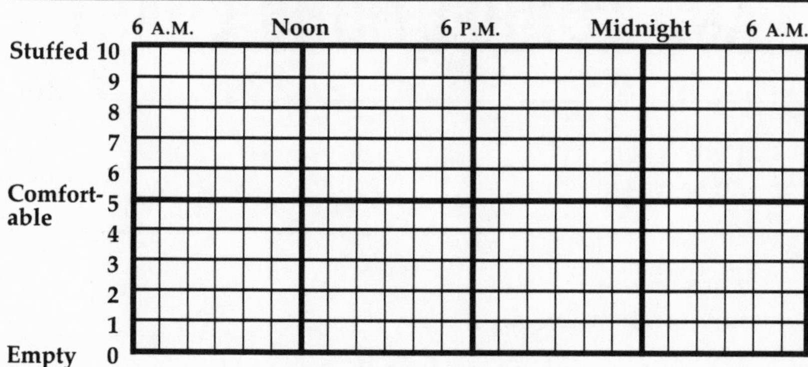

FOOD LOG

Enter all food and drink for 24 hours.	Time

THIN WITHIN OBSERVATIONS AND CORRECTIONS CHART

Observations	Day 21
1. I ate when my body was hungry.	
2. I ate in a calm environment by reducing distractions.	
3. I ate when I was sitting.	
4. I ate when my body and mind were relaxed.	
5. I ate and drank only the things my body *loved*.	
6. I paid attention only to my food while eating.	
7. I ate slowly, savoring each bite.	
8. I stopped before my body was full.	

DAY 22

A Way of Working on Miracles

Congratulations on a tremendous win! By Day 22 you have already achieved weight mastery. This means that you know how to eat as a naturally thin person throughout the ups and downs of your life. You've been doing a great job. You now know exactly what to do to put in corrections for weight mastery anytime you get off track.

All you have to do is start eating when you're at a 0 and stop at a 5 or less. Slow down when you eat, and consider the liquids you drink as part of this process. In the old days, do you remember how you *tried not* to get hungry? You were afraid you'd never stop eating once you started. So you drank a lot of water, diet drinks, or coffee, right? We had one graduate who invented her own "water diet." She drank only water all day long and said she never got hungry. However, since she denied herself food, when she got off her water fast, she swung totally the other way, binging on all the foods she had deprived herself of. This binge-deprive syndrome is well known to many of us.

In Thin Within it's just the opposite. We want to get hungry because then *we can eat anything we want!*

If you're having a little trouble recognizing what a 5 is, ask yourself the following questions:

Am I at a 0 when I start eating?

Am I drinking too much liquid?

Am I eating so fast I can't tell when I get to a 5?

The feeling of 5 is the feeling of *just enough.* It is that light, energetic feeling you have after eating exactly the right amount of food.

If you've been starting at 0 and stopping at a 5 or less since day 1 of *Thin Within* and your goal was to release excess weight, then you will have released approximately 5 pounds by now. Obviously, we don't want you to run out to the garage and pull out your dusty, rusty scale and jump on it. The point today is to focus on your results to see if you're getting what you want. It is also to start a dialogue with your body to see how much weight you've released. In order to find out, check your belt, skirt, or jeans. Are they getting looser?

Is this true for you? If you are 5 or more pounds lighter, sign your name here: ________________________

Congratulations! You have participated 100 percent and you have the results to prove it!

If you haven't released 5 or more pounds and your goal was to release excess weight, be honest with yourself and look at the results you have achieved, acknowledge yourself and sign here: ________________________

Congratulations! You're learning what works and what doesn't work! Gently forgive or commend yourself and know that today you're going to learn how to interpret your Hunger Numbers with greater accuracy so that, after observing your progress and forgiving yourself, you will be able to make more appropriate corrections. You will then start releasing weight much faster.

REFOCUSING OUR HUNGER GRAPHS

All right. Let's look now at all the numbers you've marked on your Hunger Graphs since Day 16. Now compare your numbers on the graphs with the pounds that you've released so far. If you haven't let go of at least 5 pounds so far it means very simply that you have not been eating from a 0 to 5 or less. I realize you may think you are; in fact, you may be convinced you *have* been eating 0 to 5. So for now simply consider this possibility. Looking at your graphs for the past 6 days, what corrections could you make? If, for instance, your graphs show some over-5 eating, be sure you're at a 0 when you begin to eat and that you're stopping at a 5 or less from now on. Also see if you can correct any of the situations in your life that may be stimulating your Fat Machinery.

If your graphs show a lot of 0s and 5s but you're releasing weight very slowly or not at all, then reinterpret your body's numbers, because the ones you're writing down are inaccurate.

Believe me, if you hit a clear, resounding 0 when you start eating and you stop at a 5, which is that light, energetic just-enough feeling, your excess weight will effortlessly slip away. The most probable reason for slow progress is that you're eating from a 1 to a 6 and calling it a 0 to 5. Hang in there—you'll find *your* 0 to 5. Everyone does!

Write down in the space provided what corrections you will make in order to accelerate your weight mastery.

Observations and Corrections—How I Can Accelerate My Weight Mastery

____

____

____

____

____

____

____

____

____

FORGIVENESSES AND AFFIRMATIONS

All along we have used the tools of Observations and Corrections in this process. Now, as part of your feedback, let's add to it the Forgiveness and Affirmation tools.

Today you are gearing up for the last 8 days of Thin Within. And before we move on at a faster clip, look again at your participation in this process so far. Have you done it every day? Have you used your tools faithfully. If you haven't participated 100 percent, forgive yourself in the following space for the things you haven't done in order to clean your slate and give yourself a fresh start!

Cleaning the Slate

Write the Forgiveness 10 times. An example might be, "I forgive you, ________________________ (name), for not writing your Forgivenesses."

How do you feel now? Lighter? Remember that this process of forgiveness moves us out of the suffering for the past into present time. And it is only in present time that we can experience fully that, "I *do* deserve to be thin," and feel free to commit ourselves anew to do all that is necessary to achieve the weight-mastery goals we choose for ourselves. You see, unless you forgive yourself for any lack of participation so far in this book, it, too, can become another opportunity to trigger Fat Machinery. After forgiving ourselves we return to present time, waiting once again for a 0.

When you feel you've blown it, you just get back on track by hitting 0 before you eat. And, without anger or self-recrimination, observe your behavior, forgive yourself, and put in the proper correction. Remember, we learn by our mistakes. We discover our true selves by slipping, falling, picking ourselves up, dusting ourselves off, making compassionate adjustments, and continuing on!

DESERVING TO BE THIN AFFIRMATION EXERCISES

Since the combination of forgivenesses followed by Affirmations is so powerful, continue today's cleansing exercise with a firm affirmation about deserving to have it all. After I give you a few examples, you'll write down a series of ten Affirmations, each one upping the ante of the preceding one.

Let me demonstrate. "I, Judy, deserve to be a thin person and have a whole new wardrobe."

And the affirmation that follows might be, "I, Judy, deserve not only to be a thin person and have a new wardrobe but I also deserve a gorgeous mink coat!"

So write 10 progressively wonderful Affirmations in the following space. Go for it!

Deserving-It-All Affirmations

____

____

____

Now, how do you feel? On a scale of 0 to 10, 10 being terrific, what number is that thin person within right now? You can spontaneously generate this feeling any time by using the combination of Forgivenesses and Affirmations. Forgive yourself and then affirm all the things that you want and deserve in your life.

These two tools will work in all areas of your life. If you are putting up with something that's not a terrific 10, it may be a reflection of your not believing that you deserve to have a 10. Forgivenesses followed by Affirmations, used in that order, are the tools to make your future a fantastic 10.

FINAL GOAL CONTRACTS

By doing Forgivenesses, you clean the slate. And by doing Affirmations, you write on the slate what you really want and feel you deserve. And the way to get what you deserve, step by step, is by using this next excellent tool—the Goal Contract.

In Thin Within we say that making a Goal Contract and sticking with it is a way of actualizing your miracles. I can't describe for you what your life would be like if you had it all. You must do that for yourself. Setting three realistic goals is a way for you to see how, with the correct direction and motivation, you can accomplish your own miracles. Realistic goal setting is a way to create your dreams and systematically work toward them.

These last 8 days of Thin Within are very special and a chance for you to achieve the weight-mastery goals you set for yourself. To support you I have created the Thin Within Goal

Contract that will show you a shortcut to your goals. If you stick with it, you will release more weight in the next 8 days than you ever thought possible. The exciting part is that the shortcut will be your creation. I'm just here to direct you.

First of all, understand that if you want miracles to happen it's very important to be very specific about them.

Turn back to Day 16 and look at your first goal, which is weight loss. You now have 8 days remaining. How many pounds do you realistically want to release?

Write it down under Goal #1.

THIN WITHIN GOAL CONTRACT

Date:________________________

Present weight:________________

Desired Weight:________________

How much weight will I release by Day 30? ____

Goal #1. ______________________________________

What specific actions will I take to produce the weight results I want? When will I take these actions? Let me give you some examples:

Goal #1. I will release 5 pounds by Day 30.

1. The action I'll take is to follow the Thin Within Keys to Weight Mastery 100 percent every time I choose to eat or drink for this next 8 days. To help myself I will photocopy my Observations and Corrections Chart and look at it before each meal and mark it after each meal. I'll also check through the Observations and Corrections Charts I've filled in in this book and pick out a Key to Weight Mastery that I will focus on—eating while sitting, for instance, and emphasize it every day for the next 8 days.

2. The second action I'll take to support my goal is to eat 0 to 5 or less 100 percent of the time for the next 8 days. To do this I will photocopy the Hunger Graph and carry it with me at all times. I'll choose to ride my 0 from Friday evening until Saturday noon (See Day 5 on how to do it).

3. The third action is to move my body in the most enjoyable way possible for fifteen minutes every day for the next 8 days.

4. The fourth action is to write 10 Forgivenesses on people in my Fat Story (one each day—Monday my mom, Tuesday my father, etc.) followed by 10 Affirmations: "I, ________________________, am naturally thin and use the Thin Within Keys to Weight Mastery 100 percent of the time for the next 8 days. Therefore, I will release 5 pounds effortlessly."

5. The fifth action is to do a loving, supportive thing for my body (buy myself some new underwear or cologne, enjoy a hot-tub or massage, rub lotion all over my body, etc.) each day for the next 8 days so that my body joyfully responds to my love by letting go of the 5 pounds.

These are just examples. You can do anything you want to support yourself in effortlessly reaching your weight-mastery goals. Notice how all of these things can be done in 8 days. The affirmation directly supports my goal of releasing 5 pounds by Day 30 and ensures that I will have a good time during the process. Remember, having fun is essential!

Goals #2 and #3 can be in areas that support your weight mastery such as health, fitness, appearance, environment, or correcting situations that might stimulate your Fat Machinery.

Goal #2. By Day 30, I will have my clothes closet in excellent order which will support my naturally thin self. (Notice how this goal is specific, positive, and also motivational!)

1. The action I'll take is to go through my closet on Sunday and get rid of all my fat clothes.

2. Help my friend Marge move, who will in turn support me in getting rid of my fat clothes. On Tuesday evening, we'll pack them up and cart them off to the thrift shop.

3. On Thursday I'll go window shopping to get used to trying on thin clothes, picking out things that are only pleasers.

4. Say 10 Forgivenesses and 10 Affirmations about the

new me to strengthen my belief that I deserve a totally new wardrobe.

Notice how I enlisted a friend to support me in clearing away my fat clothes? This is the Thin Within way. We didn't get fat alone nor do we get thin alone. Our graduates often use this technique of asking for support in order to complete a task. For instance, one woman wanted to discard some unpleasant reminders from her past. But every time she started to do it, she would stop to read all the letters or look through all of the picture albums, and she never completed the project. So she asked three Thin Within friends to come over, who enjoyed helping her do it.

So fill out the following Goal Contract with visions of what you know you will do in 8 days, stretching yourself a bit, and then write from four to six specific actions that you can take to get there.

THIN WITHIN GOAL CONTRACT

Weight: How much weight will I release by Day 30? (Fill in below).

Goal #1. ______________________________

What specific actions will I take to produce the weight results I want? When will I take these actions?

1. ______________________________
2. ______________________________
3. ______________________________
4. ______________________________
5. ______________________________
6. ______________________________

Goal #2. ______________________________

What specific actions will I take—and when will I take those actions—to produce the intended results?

1. ______________________________

2. ______________________________

3. ______________________________

4. ______________________________

5. ______________________________

6. ______________________________

Goal #3. ______________________________

What specific actions will I take—and when will I take those actions—to produce the intended results?

1. ______________________________

2. ______________________________

3. ______________________________

4. ______________________________

5. ______________________________

6. ______________________________

I agree to this Contract.

Signed: ______________________ Date:__________

Sign and date your Goal Contract at the bottom as a commitment to yourself that you're going to fulfill these actions in order to achieve your goals.

Read your contract every morning when you awaken and determine how to focus on it each day. At night reread it and acknowledge every win that you've made toward your goal. Forgive every loss. And ask yourself if the goal is realistic.

Finally, I'd like to point out that in fulfilling these contracts, you are calling upon the natural genius inside you which knows exactly what you need to do to achieve your goals.

SUCCESS TOOLS

• Refer to your Thin Within Goal Contract today and every day to achieve your goals.

• The miracle is that the body speaks. The key is to discern the message. Often we think it is food our body wants when actually we're thirsty. Remember you can drink water any time you want and any way you want it—walking, talking, running!

• Continue to use your Hunger Graph.

• Continue to fill in your Observations and Corrections Chart.

• Use the Thin Within Keys to Weight Mastery.

THIN WITHIN SECRET

If you want miracles
To happen
It's important for you
To be very specific about them!

HUNGER GRAPH

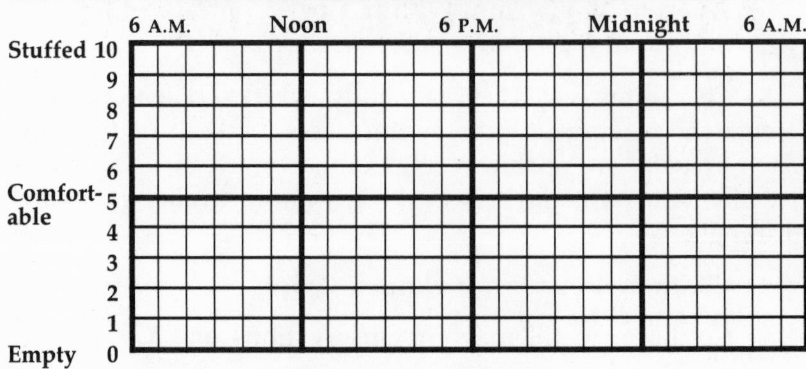

FOOD LOG

Enter all food and drink for 24 hours.	Time

THIN WITHIN OBSERVATIONS AND CORRECTIONS CHART

Observations	Day 22
1. I ate when my body was hungry.	
2. I ate in a calm environment by reducing distractions.	
3. I ate when I was sitting.	
4. I ate when my body and mind were relaxed.	
5. I ate and drank only the things my body *loved*.	
6. I paid attention only to my food while eating.	
7. I ate slowly, savoring each bite.	
8. I stopped before my body was full.	

DAY 23

Creating a Safe Place to Win

Every time you open *Thin Within* you open a reservoir of possibilities. And sometimes, especially for people who have been hiding out, this can be scary. I understand this fear. I've felt it, too. It means coming out of hibernation, telling the truth, and revealing our true selves. It's about having it all.

Our wall of fat is a way of hiding out, of protecting ourselves. I'll never forget the woman who got up in front of the workshop participants and pantomimed that she was unzipping her Fat Body and taking it off as if it were a thick winter coat. She said, "I've been terrified of doing that, afraid of how tiny I'd feel if I took off that coat of fleshy armor."

For many of us this is the reason we fail to keep the weight off. It's not only that we feel we don't deserve to have it all, but that we're afraid. We feel too vulnerable when we're thin. We feel we have too many choices. We feel we need something between us and other people. We feel afraid of having too much energy. We feel afraid that we'll get into some kind of trouble.

It is true that with every pound we release we *will* have more energy, since stored weight is stored energy. In Days 24 and 25 I will be showing you how to find new ways to use this energy to make all areas of your life 10s.

But before you can accept and use the energy effectively, you must feel comfortable with yourself. This book is your map and we have already completed 22 days of your exciting journey. But ultimately the journey will be uniquely yours. The tools of Thin Within empower you to be on your own, to do your own thing like the eagle. Do you trust yourself? Can you safely affirm that you are capable of using this energy properly, constructively, and creatively? You will want to feel that it is safe to trust your body and your heart as your own personal journey unfolds.

The way to build this safe place for yourself is through the Forgiveness and Affirmation tools. Whenever you feel afraid you can write (or say) the following Affirmations (or make up appropriate ones for yourself):

"It is now safe for me, ________________________, to be thin."

If you're not quite there yet, then this affirmation will facilitate the process:

"I, ________________________, am now willing to see that it is safe for me to be thin."

One of our graduates, Sally, who took the workshop in 1977, took five years to feel safe enough to release her entire 95 pounds. She did it slowly but surely, at her own pace, and she felt great the entire time! Toby, who I mentioned previously, on the other hand, zipped to her goal of releasing 70 pounds in just a few months. Do it at any rate you choose, remembering that you're in the driver's seat. However, constantly use Affirmations so that you will feel safe and protected as you progress. Filling your affirmations with love is what makes the process so enjoyable and effective.

I found the following Affirmations very helpful in creating safety for me.

"I, ________________________, am now naturally thin and I accept the feeling of being light and happy as my natural state."

"I, ________________________, am naturally thin and it is safe for me to feel good about myself at all times."

"I, ________________________, am naturally thin and it is totally safe for me to forgive everyone who had a part in my past Fat Story."

FREEING THE FEAR

Another way of creating safety for yourself as you release weight and pent-up energy is to stay in the present moment.

Some people are afraid to have a perfect life because they believe that such happiness is always followed by some sort of disaster. This kind of thinking isn't supportive; it is living in the past. If we stay in the present and forgive and affirm while eating 0 to 5, then we will *know* we deserve the best. I believe each of us deserves to be radiant, healthy, generous, light, and happy. Through the gift of forgiveness and affirmations we can learn to open our hands and hearts and accept all of these nurturing things. Remember, the more we conceive the more we can receive. And the more we can receive, the more we can share with others.

WINS

Thin Within is a place for winners. The question we always ask each other is, "What's working in your life?"

Instead of sitting around telling each other our sad stories and all of our problems, we:

1. Focus on our successes rather than our failures.

2. Notice what we have accomplished rather than what we have left undone.

3. See and acknowledge our beauty rather than focus on our imperfections.

4. And, finally, notice and acknowledge all the times we've used the Thin Within Keys to Weight Mastery rather than judging ourselves for the times we haven't.

In Thin Within we're always moving toward what feels good and loving, and acknowledging our wins is a splendid way of keeping our adrenaline flowing.

You see, in this book you're learning to be your own coach. As you observe and correct and look at your behavior on that TV monitor, you continue to forgive yourself and make appropriate corrections. Also commend yourself for every win you've had along the way to weight mastery. Acknowledging your day-by-day wins is as important as using Forgivenesses, Affirmations, and Visualizations in the process of changing unworkable beliefs into workable ones. It positively underlines the actions you've taken (eating 0 to 5 and using the Keys to Weight Mastery) to achieve your weight-loss goals.

THE THIN WITHIN WAY OF LIFE

The Thin Within way of life is full of opportunities rather than problems. We believe that every breakdown results in a breakthrough. Our problems with weight, food, and overeating have produced our greatest win. How? Because eating disorders led to the development of the Thin Within Keys to Weight Mastery, which, in turn, provided you with the tools to reshape all areas of your life that have been less than perfect.

We begin on the level of cause; that is, belief. And we change beliefs through Forgivenesses, Affirmations, Visualizations, Goal-Setting, and Daily Acknowledgments. And out of our new, positive beliefs—I am naturally thin and I deserve it all!—flow the perfect actions (eating 0 to 5 and all the steps you wrote in your Goal Contracts yesterday) to achieve the marvelous results that you want.

As one of our graduates says, "What I got from Thin Within is that I can have it all. All you have to do is set goals, be willing to take the responsibility for what unfolds, accept it, and joyously move forth." Another says, "You mean little ol' me—I deserve? Wooee!" And another: "I love the gratitudes most—the giving thanks for the perfect right action that unfolds."

GIVING THANKS

As that graduate said so beautifully, acknowledging our wins each and every day is a way of giving thanks for the perfect right action that flows effortlessly out of your beliefs.

So the Thin Within way of life is to begin each day with 10 written Forgivenesses and Affirmations, eating 0 to 5, all the foods your body loves, using the Thin Within Keys to Weight

Mastery, and ending each day with 10 Acknowledgment Affirmations.

Example: "I, ______________________, am naturally thin and I ______________ today" (acknowledge yourself for what you did that was a win). Anything in this process can be a win if it supports your naturally thin and radiant self.

I remember a mother telling me in a support group that a real breakthrough occurred for her when she started writing her wins (no matter how insignificant they seemed). What had happened to her was that as a housewife and a mother she thought she wasn't accomplishing much. However, when she recorded all the little things she did and acknowledged herself, she began to feel really good about herself.

The important point here is to acknowledge continually what is working in your life. This is contagious energy. Talk about your wins and you'll feel more energized and joyous every day. You have the power to choose—you can stay in the muck or get out of it. You now have the tools to do it for yourself.

THE THIN WITHIN AFFIRMATIONS

These powerful Affirmations are very effective in changing you at the belief level. Read them aloud to yourself. You can also put them on tape (with or without soft, soothing appropriate music) and play them as often as possible.

When you read or listen to them, relax in a chair . . . let go of any tensions . . . take a deep breath and close your eyes . . . let yourself go back to the beautiful open space where you created your Thin Self. . . . Get a clear picture in your mind of your beautiful open space . . . once again see your Thin Self . . . become your Thin Self . . . enjoy your Thin Self . . . move in your beautiful green open space . . . experience the feeling of lightness and joy right now as your Thin Self moves . . . now open your eyes and read each of these phrases slowly out loud:

1. I know the issue of weight is solvable in my life.

2. I know I can free myself of excess weight and achieve my natural size.

3. I know I deserve to manifest on the outside the magnificence I am on the inside.

4. I am a naturally thin person. I think as a thin person thinks. I eat as a thin person eats. Therefore, I have a thin body.

5. I acknowledge myself for being willing to do whatever I have to do to reach and maintain my natural size.

6. I affirm my ability to eat according to the Thin Within Keys to Weight Mastery.

7. I recognize the signals my body sends me regarding its needs, and I respect and honor those signals.

8. I eat only when my body is hungry.

9. I eat while sitting down in a peaceful environment.

10. I eat selectively, only the foods I love.

11. I eat slowly and savor each bite of my food.

12. My body tells me when it's satisfied and I respectfully stop eating.

13. I willingly and joyfully leave food on my plate.

14. I lovingly forgive my actions as I observe and correct, redirecting my energy in positive and constructive ways.

15. I know I can maintain my natural size through the ups and downs of my life.

16. Each day my body comes closer to reflecting on the outside the magnificence I am on the inside.

17. I am a naturally thin person. I think as a thin person thinks. I eat as a thin person eats. Therefore, I have a thin body.

18. I am a thin person. I *am* a thin person.

SUCCESS TOOLS

• Create new, interesting ways that show your body you love it and that it is safe for it to blossom. Take it for a brisk walk, breathe deeply the fresh air, give it the gift of a massage or a swim, cover it with colorful clothes. Talk to it often with loving affirmations. This is how you make it safe for you and your body to be on the same team.

• The environment (home, work, and recreation) we create for ourselves should provide safe nesting places in which our bodies can brood (what a wonderful word—it means gestation) and blossom. Surround yourself with things that allow you to feel loved, acknowledged, and affirmed.

• Continue to use your Hunger Graph.

• Use the Keys to Weight Mastery.

• Mark your Observations and Corrections Chart.

THIN WITHIN SECRET

Life was meant to be a mystery.
To be lived spontaneously
From a present time,
Unpredictable place.

HUNGER GRAPH

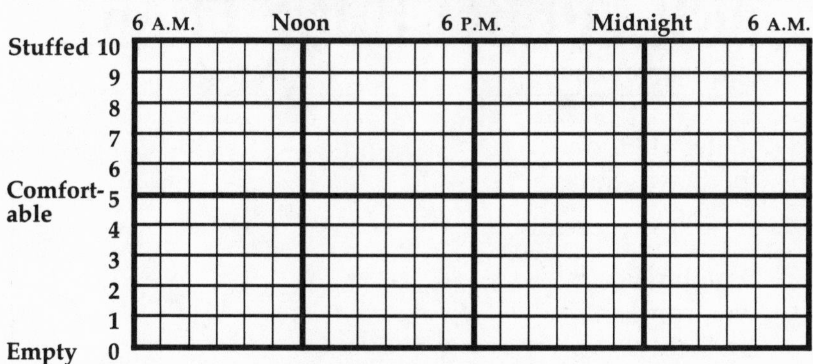

FOOD LOG

Enter all food and drink for 24 hours.	Time

THIN WITHIN OBSERVATIONS AND CORRECTIONS CHART

Observations	Day 23
1. I ate when my body was hungry.	
2. I ate in a calm environment by reducing distractions.	
3. I ate when I was sitting.	
4. I ate when my body and mind were relaxed.	
5. I ate and drank only the things my body *loved*.	
6. I paid attention only to my food while eating.	
7. I ate slowly, savoring each bite.	
8. I stopped before my body was full.	

DAY 24

Thin People Live in the Fast Lane

Recently I went jogging with an old friend who isn't involved in Thin Within. As we jogged along she told me one "ain't it awful" story after another. Afterward she said, "Eleven thirty A.M.! Oh boy! Only thirty minutes until it's time to eat. Something to look forward to—lunch!"

As I listened to her I remembered how it used to be for me. There were times when I had nothing to look forward to except my sad life and one meal after another. I lived from snack to snack. Food was an obsession and a total preoccupation. Have you ever considered how much time we spend on our obsession with food, our bodies, and our weight?

After working with thousands of people I've concluded that Americans spend approximately eight to ten hours a day in their obsession with food and eating. Has this been true for you?

Now that you have the tools for weight mastery, how many hours in a day does it take to ask your body if it is hungry, eat from 0 to 5 or less, and follow the Thin Within Keys to Weight Mastery? Let's say you now spend approximately two hours a day being concerned with food, eating, and weight mastery. That means you have freed up six to eight hours!

You've freed up not only energy but time as well. A lot of

time! What we're going to be discussing in the last 3 days of *Thin Within* is how to use this time effectively, turning problems that grip us into projects that serve us.

DEFINITIONS OF ENERGY

Remember that fat is stored energy, and it represents additional mass. Science tells us that your body needs extra energy to metabolize and move that additional mass. So as you release the extra mass that was a burden to your body, your body will then become an even more efficient system. I believe that the uniqueness of each of us is represented by an intricate mass-energy interplay that is directed and controlled by the mind, and that the ultimate architecture of our body is determined by our thoughts. In the past 23 days you have been reshaping your form. You have been creating yourself through the use of Forgivenesses, Affirmations, Visualizations, and Daily Acknowledgments. You've been learning how to handle one of the biggest problems in your life— your obsession with eating, food, weight. Now you have tools to use in many situations to stay naturally slim—hit a 0, eat to a 5 or less, watch your Fat Machinery, observe and correct, forgive and affirm. That's it! You have it!

What we want to do now is to show you how to apply these same tools to help you make all areas of your life 10s. You see, I believe you deserve it *all*. And if you're doing your forgivenesses and affirmations every day, you're beginning to *believe* it also! One after another of our graduates has released the weight and changed his or her life. Barbara Bernard quit her job and started her own successful business. Ann Lockward let go of 10 pounds and released so much energy she doubled her salary. This release of energy doesn't necessarily mean you will make major changes in your life. When Nan Taralini came to us she was a Salvation Army minister. She thought that in order to get thin she'd have to quit her job because she was fed up with it and was overeating because of it. But the problem was that if she quit, her husband, who dearly loved the Army, would have to quit, too. After Thin Within she discovered a new definition of forgiveness that freed her up to perceive all the beauty, depth, and goodness in her life. Now she can see her job is a 10 and she has reached her desired weight.

MASTERY OVER LIFE

Ask yourself if you are as willing to fill your life with possibility, contribution, success, joy, and love as you are to slim down to your marvelously svelte body. If you could write the script for all aspects of your life, what would it be like? Let's do some dreaming. This isn't like setting goals as we did on Day 3, because there is no commitment. You will merely ask, What if . . .? Make sure that each of your answers to the questions below represents a 10. Remember, you already are a miracle—you have successfully resolved your food and eating problems—and now we're going to produce other miracles in your life.

Discovering New Possibilities in My Life

1. If I could have my work any way I want it, what would it be like?

____

____

____

2. If I could have my friendships any way I wanted them, how would they be?

____

____

____

3. If I could have a perfect relationship with my family, what would it be like?

4. If my financial situation were a total pleaser, how would it be?

5. If I could have the world and my contribution to it any way I wanted, what would it be like?

6. If I could have a perfect body, what would it be like?

7. If all my possessions were perfect, what would I have (home, car, clothes, etc.)?

You've just created a version of what you'd like your successful life to be like. Tomorrow we're going to discuss how you can have it and what Thin Within's version of a successful person is.

SUCCESS TOOLS

• Today you'll be using a tool that will strengthen your resolve in the Belief ⟶Action ⟶Result exercise discussed on Day 20. During the day talk to yourself, to your mirror, to your friends, etc., about your naturally thin self:

> "I am such a thin person that I'm simply not interested in second helpings."
>
> "I am such a thin person that I'm too busy to eat."
>
> "I am such a thin person I can take food or leave it."
>
> "Every day I am coming closer to my weight goal, easily and effortlessly."
>
> "I am such a thin person I listen to my body and I do what my body asks of me."

• Affirm your ability to follow the Thin Within Keys to Weight Mastery. Say them boldly out loud (no fair mumbling into your pillow or just thinking them).

• Talk to five different people (one each day until Day 29) about your experience of your Thin Self. It can be anyone—you don't even have to know them! One of my favorite stories is about a woman in a very crowded elevator. As she got off she turned back to the crowd and said proudly, "Do you know why we were all able to fit in this elevator? Because I'm a naturally thin person, that's why!"

• Continue to move your body fifteen minutes each day in the most loving manner possible.

• Continue to mark the Hunger Graph.

• Fill in the Observations and Corrections Chart.

• Use the Thin Within Keys to Weight Mastery.

THIN WITHIN SECRET

Fill your body and
Fill your life
With what you love
And you'll stay
Naturally thin.

HUNGER GRAPH

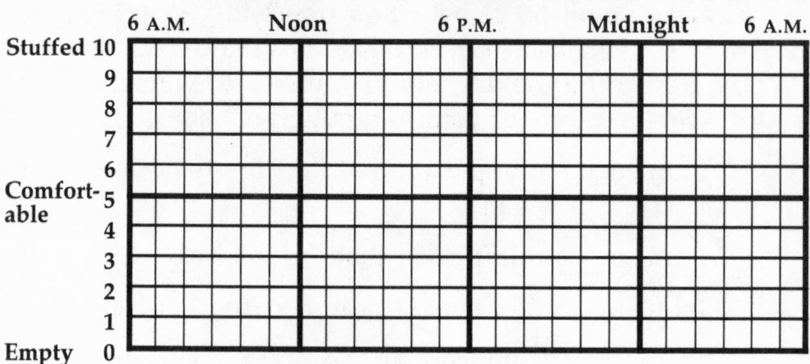

FOOD LOG

Enter all food and drink for 24 hours.	Time

THIN WITHIN OBSERVATIONS AND CORRECTIONS CHART

Observations	Day 24
1. I ate when my body was hungry.	
2. I ate in a calm environment by reducing distractions.	
3. I ate when I was sitting.	
4. I ate when my body and mind were relaxed.	
5. I ate and drank only the things my body *loved*.	
6. I paid attention only to my food while eating.	
7. I ate slowly, savoring each bite.	
8. I stopped before my body was full.	

DAY 25

Creating Myself Anew

Our lives either support or hinder our weight mastery. Now that we have the tools to handle our weight problem we have, as was pointed out yesterday, freed up a lot of time and energy. How we use this time and energy will largely determine whether we keep the weight off permanently. Problems are the main triggers for our Fat Machinery and if this newly released time were to fill up with such things as nonsupportive relationships, our Fat Machinery might again be activated. In other words, we will want to surround ourselves more and more with winners as we get rid of more and more losers.

Yesterday's exercise, creating your ideal life, was an important first step in allowing you to see not only what is deficient or missing in your life, but how changing your beliefs can start the process of replacing losers with winners.

In order to change beliefs, to get into that fast lane, we need to understand that the way we achieve success as a naturally thin person is very different from how we have done it in the past.

Success involves opening up possibilities for ourselves and others. It produces harmony between work and play, excitement and serenity. It does not include going off the deep end. Cynthia Martin realized during her Thin Within experience that the reason her life wasn't working was because it consisted of too much superficial gratification and no deep satisfaction. Tom Blacksmith was very satisfied with one aspect of his life (he was a millionaire), but he was disappointed in another area because he had never learned how to have fun without eating and was 125 pounds overweight when he came to Thin Within.

A LIFE FULL OF SATISFACTION

A life full of satisfaction is one in which what you do comes from within and involves a successful relationship with yourself—one in which all the results are earned. Satisfaction is knowing deep down inside that you have kept your promises, have pressed yourself beyond your comfort zone, and have participated 100 percent.

We've all had experiences that made us very happy about ourselves, because we knew, in our hearts, how hard we had worked and that we deserved our success. In other words, we earned it. What a marvelous feeling it is to complete a deeply satisfying job. To work 100 percent, keep our agreements, and press ourselves. It's that deep sigh of yes, thank you, it's over, and I did my very best.

Let's again examine those seven important areas in your life. Yesterday we looked at the ideal—what you would have if there were no limitations. You *can* change your life, so today we want to look at reality. Start by asking yourself if there is anything missing in each area. What could be added (or subtracted) that would satisfy you in a deep and meaningful way. Write your answers in the spaces provided.

Seven Important Areas

1. Work

____

____

____

____

2. Relationships

3. Family

4. My body

5. Possessions

6. Finances

7. Contributions to the world

____

____

____

____

In order to sustain our naturally thin selves there needs to be a balance between working hard for the things we genuinely believe in and relaxing and enjoying the pleasures in life. Being a workaholic or being completely without purpose in our lives stimulates Fat Machinery.

We need to work and play, to enjoy and feel pain. We need to experience the freshness of nature, the joy of creativity, the ecstasy and power of love, the satisfaction of hard manual labor, and the serenity that comes from a satisfying relationship with God.

Here are four steps to support and help you in your quest for more satisfaction in your life.

1. *Be responsible.* When you make an agreement with yourself to complete something, *do it*! Follow through, finish it. The secret is to work as hard for *yourself* as you do for others!

2. *Make choices that serve you.* Ask yourself if this is what you really want. Is this true satisfaction for you? A pleaser? What does your body want right now? What does your heart want?

3. *Be unreasonable.* Ask yourself to what extent you are willing to go in order to get the results you want. This means doing what your heart of hearts wants you to do. It means speaking up for what you really want no matter how unreasonable it may seem. It means writing Forgivenesses and Affirmations that support: "I deserve to be who and what I really am." It means doing more loving things for yourself when the chips are down. And it means not abusing your body by overeating.

4. *Get results.* You can do more than just talk about your dreams. *You can set goals and achieve them*! Let go of all that weight you said you wanted to release. Return to Day 24 and look at your dreams. You now have all the tools necessary to achieve these goals. Reward yourself as you progress along the way. You deserve it!

CREATIVE SOLUTIONS EXERCISE

Finally, in order to support you in your quest for more satisfaction, here is an exercise that will allow you to get in touch with all of the incompletions in your life that have kept you from being a total success. We do this for a very simple reason—incompletions can and do stimulate Fat Machinery. Also, avoiding incompletions prevents us from being in present time. By clearing them up we free ourselves to concentrate on more rewarding things in our lives. So complete them rather than eat because of them. Take a couple of minutes and list below the things you've been avoiding in your life. Your list may include something as banal as cleaning your oven or as complex as calling a sibling you haven't talked to in five years. Now fill out the columns on the right side which indicate how and when you will complete the items on your list.

Things I've Been Avoiding	Creative Solutions (how and when I'm going to complete them)

SUCCESS TOOLS

• Being totally satisfied makes all areas of your life more rewarding. As you progress toward your weight goal, remember that where the mind sells out is to the familiar instead of the unfamiliar. In Thin Within, we call this our "yabut." "Yabut I'm afraid to reach my desired weight. . . . Yabut I can't even imagine having all pleasers in all areas of my life. . . ." Yabut is the voice in the mind that sells out. Thank your yabut for sharing, put in a correction, and continue waiting for your 0 while redirecting your energy into other, more satisfying areas of your life!

• Speak your Affirmations out loud.

• Continue marking Hunger Graph.

• Continue to fill in the Observations and Corrections Chart.

• Use the Thin Within Keys to Weight Mastery.

THIN WITHIN SECRET

The way to experience more
Satisfaction in your life
Is to be willing to experience
The unfamiliar and
Stay in present time!

HUNGER GRAPH

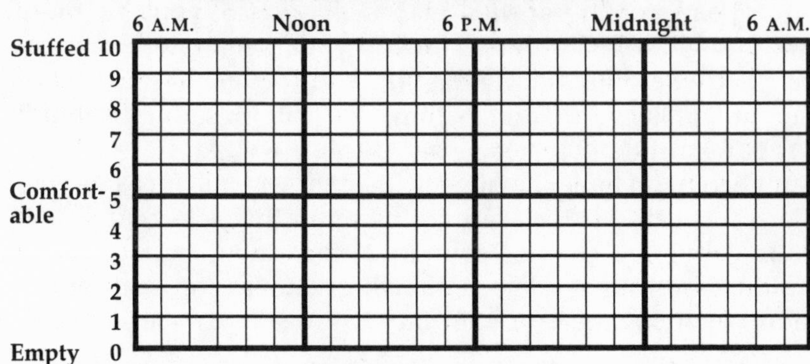

FOOD LOG

Enter all food and drink for 24 hours.	Time

THIN WITHIN OBSERVATIONS AND CORRECTIONS CHART

Observations	Day 25
1. I ate when my body was hungry.	
2. I ate in a calm environment by reducing distractions.	
3. I ate when I was sitting.	
4. I ate when my body and mind were relaxed.	
5. I ate and drank only the things my body *loved*.	
6. I paid attention only to my food while eating.	
7. I ate slowly, savoring each bite.	
8. I stopped before my body was full.	

DAY 26

How to Have a Good Time and Stay Naturally Slim

A question I frequently ask myself is "How can I have fun doing this?" I think less drudgery means more satisfaction in our lives, and almost any situation can be made more enjoyable (and more fun) if we will simply explore the possibilities. Of course, the more successful we become at this the less our Fat Machinery will be triggered, and the less we will overeat. Said in another way, when our Fat Machinery is stimulated we know that something in our life is not supporting or working for us. Something is out of whack.

Fortunately we now have the tools, the built-in mechanisms to recognize such situations, forgive ourselves (or others), put in proper corrections, and continue toward the goals which will make our lives total 10s.

HEAVY LIVES

In Thin Within we believe that heavy lives make us heavy. That's why we ask, "How can we have fun here?" If thinness is your goal then the more pleasure and fun you have, the faster you'll get there. By *pleasure* we mean all forms of gratification in your life. Gratification is absolutely necessary in order for us to succeed in life. It is very different from satisfaction, which is earned and comes from within, when we make and keep our commitments and have successful relationships with ourselves.

Gratification, on the other hand, is pleasure that comes from outside ourselves and is not necessarily earned. Gratification provides us with immediate (and temporary) pleasures—a movie, TV, food, compliments, gambling, vacations, getting a tan, etc.

HUMMINGBIRDS

What creates everlasting thinness is a harmony in our lives between satisfaction and gratification. This is because, when we feel we're not producing enough *satisfaction* in our lives, we mistakenly look for it in food. So, too, when we're over-involved with satisfaction without enough *gratification*, we'll mistakenly look for our pleasures in food. If we enjoy sufficient satisfaction and schedule gratifications along the way, our lives will be full enough that we won't feel the compulsion to "reward" ourselves with food when things are less than perfect. Then 0 to 5 eating is truly effortless. In some ways we're like hummingbirds who constantly need nectar for sustenance. Personally, as I wrote this book I enjoyed massages, the music I love, and invigorating morning walks. I scheduled my gratifications so that I would be able to keep pressing myself to complete this most satisfying and challenging project!

To me it's like planting a garden. There is satisfaction in getting the hard earth ready, planting, fertilizing, mulching, watering, and protecting the seeds so they can grow. . . . There is wonderful gratification in picking the flowers, the joy of sharing them with friends, the pleasure of bright blue irises and orange daffodils in a crystal vase. Our life needs both satisfaction and gratification to have serenity. One of the ways, however, that we sabotage ourselves is by procrastination. So in order to support you to get more fun out of your life and pleasure yourself to natural slimness, we'll look at the trouble it causes.

Procrastination is similar to the issue of satisfaction and gratification in that it very much has to do with our attitude. However, it is different in that it is definitely a trigger for Fat Machinery. Take a few minutes and list all the wonderful ways you procrastinate. You know what I mean—all the ways that you "try" to get out of walking the dog, watering the plants, mowing the lawn, cleaning the house, etc. Write whatever comes to mind. Take approximately two minutes and be creative.

How I Procrastinate

____

____

____

____

____

____

____

____

____

____

____

____

____

____

Did you have eating on your list? You can, with great delight, cross that off. If you didn't have it on your list, acknowledge yourself for a true win.

Now let's consider some new and interesting ways to procrastinate. For instance, why not explore different parts of your city or town, daydream, test-drive a new car, contemplate a new hobby, wander through a museum, sightsee, plan a trip, learn to paint, practice a musical instrument, read a good novel, move your furniture, look for a new hairstyle, dream about a new wardrobe. The list is endless. In the space below make your own list.

Creative Procrastination List

(Or, How I Can Have Fun!)

____

____

____

____

____

____

____

____

____

____

____

____

____

____

The main point is to give yourself permission to do it. It is okay to have fun in present time. There is no need to feel guilty anymore. Remember, guilt is the most fattening thing there is! It stimulates Fat Machinery which drives us to the refrigerator! Thin Within advocates enjoying deeply satisfying activities and scheduling rest and recreation as you go along. So don't feel guilty if you find yourself on the couch leafing through a magazine looking at new hairstyles. Enjoy yourself! Life is about joy and work, pleasure and pain and, of course, they are not mutually exclusive. The ebb and flow of our lives is the vital nutrient that allows us to grow. So give yourself permission to have a good time!

START A GAMEPLAN

On Day 24 you visualized the infinite possibilities for your life, and on Day 25 you listed some realistic goals for yourself. You have begun the process of freeing up the time and energy necessary to realize these goals. This is an ideal visualization, as powerful as the one you did when you broke through your wall of fat and discovered your naturally thin self waiting for you. . . . Go back to Day 24 whenever you want a booster shot, remembering that your options are constantly changing. Just keep asking yourself questions, remembering that listening to your answers is a way of hearing the new, untapped possibilities.

On Day 25 you found out that the way to become a successful thin person living in the fast lane is to be absolutely honest with and true to yourself. Starting today with your vision of what is missing from those seven important areas, you can write a script for yourself to achieve satisfaction in all of them. Tomorrow we'll talk about how to press yourself beyond the comfort zone (take heart, it can be fun) to achieve all that you want in your life. Now *you* have *all* the tools, the mastery, the energy, and the time to create your new life. Don't attempt to do it all at once. Set up a schedule that will move you directly toward your 10s. And have a good time all along the way. That's how we stay thin. We don't stay thin by creating scarcity and deprivation. (That's why diets don't work.) The key is harmony, serenity, and balance. You can have it all by setting up your gameplan.

SET UP A GAMEPLAN FOR LIFE MASTERY

1. Begin by picking (in addition to your weight goal) two goals that will produce satisfaction for you (refer to Days 24 and 25). Use the Thin Within Goal Contract as your guide. Make and keep agreements with yourself (use Day 27—Beyond Your Comfort Zone—as a guide).

2. Start today!

3. Acknowledge your *progress* with each thing you do.

4. Intersperse your time with creative procrastinations that are on purpose (meaning they support rather than hinder your satisfactions). You require rest and recreation. Work creatively and productively, then play some, and keep it up!

That's the secret of achieving all that your heart desires. Being gentle and supportive with ourselves cannot lead to abuse. "Will I love myself more" if I relax a bit and then go back to work? If the answer is yes, treat yourself. We have so much energy when we're taking care of ourselves. After we have taken care of ourselves there will be plenty of energy (and love) left, which will overflow to others.

SUCCESS TOOLS

• Some Thin Within graduates keep a Rest and Recreation List of fun things to do so they always have a creative procrastination readily available.

• Say Affirmations out loud about your naturally thin self.

• Continue to use your Hunger Graph.

• Continue to mark the Observations and Corrections Chart.

• Use the Thin Within Keys to Weight Mastery.

THIN WITHIN SECRET

Maintain a balance of satisfaction/gratification.
It raises self-esteem.
It minimizes Fat Machinery.
It supports you in your weight-mastery goal!

HUNGER GRAPH

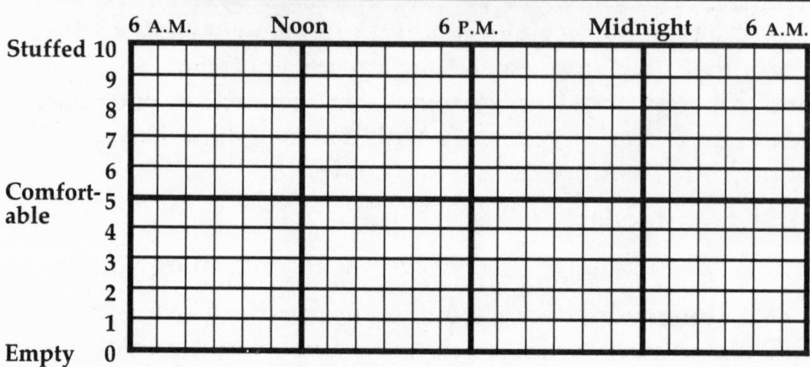

FOOD LOG

Enter all food and drink for 24 hours.	Time

THIN WITHIN OBSERVATIONS AND CORRECTIONS CHART

Observations	Day 26
1. I ate when my body was hungry.	
2. I ate in a calm environment by reducing distractions.	
3. I ate when I was sitting.	
4. I ate when my body and mind were relaxed.	
5. I ate and drank only the things my body *loved*.	
6. I paid attention only to my food while eating.	
7. I ate slowly, savoring each bite.	
8. I stopped before my body was full.	

DAY 27

Beyond Your Comfort Zone

In order to get what we really want we sometimes have to put ourselves over the line—to go beyond what we thought was possible. This is what I mean when I say press yourself beyond your comfort zone.

Counting today you have 4 days left, so let's experience what it feels like to go beyond the comfort zone. This means, first of all, that in the next 4 days you will allow yourself to experience hunger. At the same time allow yourself to feel all your feelings. Before *Thin Within* you *ate* your feelings. Now you will begin to *feel* your feelings and do something positive about them rather than to eat unconsciously because of your Fat Machinery.

ALLOW YOURSELF TO BE UNCOMFORTABLE

How often have you stopped or given up when the going got tough? How many times have you said, "I can't do it because it's too uncomfortable"? Going beyond your comfort zone means allowing yourself to be uncomfortable. . . . It means staying conscious in the present time. Indeed, in order to release all our excess weight we need to stay conscious and press ourselves beyond what we think is enough.

This is true in all areas of life. The same mechanism that

stops you with food stops you as well in relationships, money, career, sex, etc. Isn't this true?

We commonly press ourselves beyond the comfort zone for others, in our work, in relationships, or for our families. But we rarely do it for ourselves. *This last 4 days is the time to go all out for ourselves!*

A STEP BEYOND SAFE

Today you're taking the step beyond safe. That's the stretch. It may not feel comfortable and it takes faith, but that's the adventure and that's the path to progress.

We fail because we unconsciously settle for less than a 10. Look at your body, your hair, your clothes, your fingernails! Look at your job, your relationships, your family, your bureau drawers! Are they all 10s? You have been given all the tools you need, as of today, to make yourself and your environment into a 10. This doesn't mean setting out to make everyone like you. Not at all. In fact we can't really change anyone but ourselves. We make our relationships 10s by Forgivenesses and Affirmations and by telling the whole truth on a moment-to-moment basis. Here are nine basic steps that will help you go beyond your comfort zone to press for 10s.

1. *Experience Hunger.* Allow yourself truly to hit a 0 and eat to a 5 or less and miracles will occur.

2. *Stay in Present Time.* Take one day at a time and see what a radiant person you become.

3. *Do It for Yourself.* You can't do it for anyone but yourself. Continually ask the question: "Will I love myself more if I do this?" You deserve to be all that you want to be. Make a commitment to press yourself to discover who you are!

4. *Free Yourself from Unworkable Beliefs.* What beliefs do you have today that are getting in your way? Change those beliefs first by forgiving yourself and then by making an appropriate affirmation: "I, ________________________, deserve to be all that I can be, and it feels good to press myself beyond my comfort zone."

5. *Use the Observations and Corrections Tools.* This is a practical approach that works. It's about progress, not perfection. At each moment you observe your unworkable behavior, forgive yourself and put in a correction. In order to have it all, you must learn from your ups and downs.

6. *Use Forgivenesses.* When you catch yourself manifesting unconscious behavior, don't abuse yourself. Simply ask if you have bitten off more than you can chew, or if you tried to work too fast. Stretching yourself does not mean you have to feel like you're at your first day of an aerobics class! Rather it is a gentle stretch, a tender press which will inspire you to respond to the corrections you make.

7. *Use Acknowledgments.* As you go beyond your comfort zone to achieve the goals you have set for yourself, pat yourself on the back. Be pleased with your wins and tell yourself so!

8. *Get Support Wherever Possible.* You are not in this alone. You can reach out and accept or give support every step of the way. Also, you can learn from watching other people press themselves. It's like running with someone and finding that your pace has quickened because of the way that person runs.

9. *Keep Agreements with Yourself.* You keep agreements with everyone else. Now it's time to recognize that you deserve to keep agreements with yourself. You can also ask the support of others to help in doing this.

These nine steps really will help you to achieve all that you want. When I started dancing I pressed myself beyond my comfort zone at every turn. I did things I couldn't imagine myself doing. And the only reason I was able to do them was because of my belief that I was a dancer. Yet it took me years to realize that I could apply these principles to all areas of my life, including weight mastery.

Finally, you are embarked on a great adventure to become your most beautiful (or handsome), creative, and successful self. Allow yourself to complete the journey and discover yourself at the end of the story. Let yourself reach your weight-mastery goals and you will have more than enough energy to achieve all the satisfactions and gratifications you desire. You deserve them! In Thin Within we say come from within and you will stay naturally thin.

You deserve only 10s in your life—your body, your work, and your love. To accomplish this you must come from the heart—and that will set you free. You won't eat out of Fat Machinery anymore because you will finally be receiving what you deserve.

What is the Thin Within way of life? Stay conscious beyond your comfort zone and press to a 10.

SUCCESS TOOLS

- Photocopy the nine steps that will take you beyond your comfort zone and carry them with you, referring to them often. They'll support you!
- At this evening's meal choose to eat only one item, or to experience hunger and drink only liquids.
- Continue your spoken Affirmations.
- Continue to mark your Hunger Graph.
- Continue to fill in your Observations and Corrections Chart.
- Use the Thin Within Keys to Weight Mastery.

THIN WITHIN SECRET

Live your satisfactions and gratifications
And along the way
When you're at 0
Choose a pleaser
And eat to a comfortable 5 or less.

HUNGER GRAPH

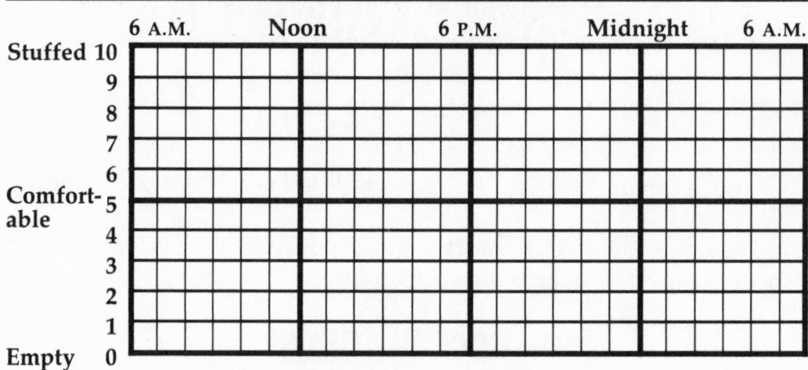

FOOD LOG

Enter all food and drink for 24 hours.	Time

THIN WITHIN OBSERVATIONS AND CORRECTIONS CHART

Observations	Day 27
1. I ate when my body was hungry.	
2. I ate in a calm environment by reducing distractions.	
3. I ate when I was sitting.	
4. I ate when my body and mind were relaxed.	
5. I ate and drank only the things my body *loved*.	
6. I paid attention only to my food while eating.	
7. I ate slowly, savoring each bite.	
8. I stopped before my body was full.	

DAY 28

How to Party with Your Thin Self

My sincere desire is to have *Thin Within* help you set up a game plan for all areas of your life. In the next 3 days we are going to discuss how problems present opportunities for creative solutions. Problems will become projects and breakdowns will become breakthroughs. Eating-related disorders are a good example of a breakdown and this book of a breakthrough. Because of your problem you bought this book and were introduced to Thin Within. This led you to a great possession—a series of tools that will serve you all the days of your life, not only to maintain your naturally slim body but also to promote an incredible life that you may not have believed you deserved.

So today we will focus on how to plan ahead for a life that will support your thin self.

PLANNING A GOOD TIME!

Think of a typical social gathering—a business lunch, a cocktail party, a dinner, or an evening with a loved one or a friend. Who and what does it involve for you? What type of food is served? Write down all the fears and obstacles that might stimulate Fat Machinery and make it seem difficult for you to eat 0 to 5. Don't write in the solution area yet; simply list the potential obstacles.

Potential Obstacles	Solutions
Abundance of food	
Too many varieties to choose from	
Nothing to wear	
Too busy	

Okay. Let's say that some of your obstacles are too much food, too much variety, drinking too much alcohol, nothing to wear, nervousness, boredom.

Suppose your biggest worry is having nothing to wear. This concern can become a tremendous opportunity for you. One of the things that has supported me in eating 0 to 5 at all times is that I make an effort to look my best. I find a pleaser (borrow or buy it) and I wear it. Then my self-esteem is so high and I'm feeling so good I don't overeat. So convert the problem of "nothing to wear" into a fun project that will result in your having an outfit that will guarantee success for the present and future outings. Another obstacle—the variety of food—can become an opportunity. The more food types, the greater the chances that your pleasers will be there! Be very selective. I first check out all the food, pick only those pleasers I really want, and I eat only those, slowly and consciously.

Now answer each of your problems with a creative solution.

The second and very important part of this exercise is to ask yourself, "What is *my* purpose in going to this particular social occasion? What do I really want to get out of it?" It's doubtful that your answer will be to overeat.

My Purpose in Going to this Social Occasion

1. To meet someone special
2. Make new acquaintances
3. Fun
4. Business contacts
5. ____________________
6. ____________________
7. ____________________
8. ____________________

After answering this question regarding your purpose you may discover that you really don't want to go at all or that eating is the last priority. In Thin Within we say there are always creative options. Be unreasonable! Would you rather go roller skating? Have a scavenger hunt? Fix a delightful dish for a friend in need? Paint the kitchen? Stay home?

In any such situation you can arrange it so that *you* win. Such wins come from the belief, "I do deserve." Creatively solving your problems is the essence of *Thin Within.* You are learning how to solve your problems yourself! You have all the tools you need!

GOODBYE TO MY FAT SELF

Now it's time to say goodbye, totally and irrevocably, to someone who in some respects has actually been very supportive in some areas of your life. Your Fat Self protected you, cushioned you, and kept you hidden. Now you don't need that "help" anymore. Say a fond goodbye to that part of you. Acknowledge your Fat Self and let it go . . . forever. I'm sure you realize the energy and emotion you invested in your Fat

Self. It's time to release that investment and put it into your successful Thin Self. That's why this letter is so important. Be creative and complete. Here's my goodbye letter.

Dear Beloved Fat Self,

Thank you for your love and devotion enough to die and let me live. You suffered so much and you tried so hard. It has been such a struggle, the desperate efforts for control, the painful self-abuse, and the torment of self-recrimination.

I know you only wanted to protect me, and you did a brilliant job; however, I can and will protect myself, and I'm ever grateful for your devotion to me. You always did exactly what I asked even though I was unaware of my requests at times.

Thank you, dear friend, for caring so much, enough to let go. I'll never forget you. We are together always in memory.

Judy Wardell

Goodbye Letter to My Fat Self

____

____

____

____

____

____

____

____

____

____

____

____

____

____

SUCCESS TOOLS

• You don't ever again have to feel like a victim at a party or a dinner. You now know you have a myriad of choices.

• Continue to do Affirmations out loud.

• Continue to use your Hunger Graph.

• Continue to fill in your Observations and Corrections Chart.

• Use the Thin Within Keys to Weight Mastery.

THIN WITHIN SECRET

The bottom line
In making any relationship a 10
Is love, forgiveness,
And acknowledgment.

HUNGER GRAPH

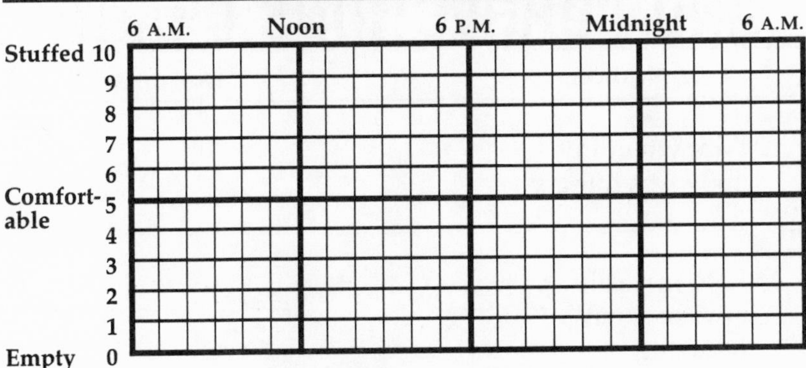

FOOD LOG

Enter all food and drink for 24 hours.	Time

THIN WITHIN OBSERVATIONS AND CORRECTIONS CHART

Observations	Day 28
1. I ate when my body was hungry.	
2. I ate in a calm environment by reducing distractions.	
3. I ate when I was sitting.	
4. I ate when my body and mind were relaxed.	
5. I ate and drank only the things my body *loved*.	
6. I paid attention only to my food while eating.	
7. I ate slowly, savoring each bite.	
8. I stopped before my body was full.	

DAY 29

How to Raise a Naturally Thin Family

Most of our mothers and fathers believed that we had to eat everything on our plates. The good kid licked his plate clean; the bad kid refused to eat certain foods. And we all know what happened—the good kid often grew up fat and the bad kid remained thin. I've heard this many, many times in the past ten years.

You may feel that bringing up a family using the Thin Within Keys to Weight Mastery and eating only pleasers 0 to 5 might present a lot of difficulties. My answer to your concern will again take the form of an exercise in which you will creatively solve some problems for yourself.

First I'd like to reiterate a few basic Thin Within priciples. Your body is a perfect instrument. If you listen to it rather than your Fat Machinery, it will tell you what you need to eat to stay healthy. This isn't just a Thin Within belief. A number of experiments done over the years validate what is termed the conveyor-belt theory of nutrition. If you allow children to choose from a wide variety of foods they will generally choose only sweets for the first few days. Very quickly, however, they begin listening to their bodies, noticing how their bodies respond to so much sugar, and, after a few days, start choosing healthy foods.

One of our Thin Within graduates experienced a very dramatic illustration of this principle. She was severely anemic after donating a large portion of her bone marrow to her brother who was dying of leukemia. She was given pills to build up her blood, but she stopped them because they nauseated her. The doctor told her that this might occur and recommended eating while taking the medication. However, this threw her Hunger Numbers off. So she stopped taking the pills and, instead, asked her body what it really wanted. The answer was rice, raisins, half-and-half, steak, and cheese, and her blood count rapidly returned to normal while on this regimen.

EATING THE THIN WITHIN WAY WITH MY FAMILY EXERCISES

Think of a typical meal with your family. Who and what does it involve for you? What type of food is usually served? What obstacles get in the way of your family eating the Thin Within way? Write down all that come to mind. Don't write the solutions yet.

Potential Obstacles	Solutions
Every child has a different pleaser.	
My husband comes home and wants to eat and I don't.	

Okay. Now write the true reasons you eat with others—your family, husband, roommate, etc.

My Purpose in Eating with Someone Else

1. Hunger
2. Conversation
3. Convenience
4. ____________________
5. ____________________
6. ____________________

The reason for determining *why* you eat with someone else is that it will help you to create the solutions that will remove those obstacles. When Don and Carol Wiseman finally realized they could sit and talk with their children at the dinner table without having to eat with them, their relationship with the children vastly improved. Knowing that children will instinctively eat nutritiously if allowed to choose from a variety of foods means they no longer nag at the kids about what they do (or don't) eat. This makes the experience much more pleasant and meaningful for everyone.

Cynthia Martin lets each of her three children pick one pleaser each night from one of the four food groups, so, even though they don't have *all* of their pleasers at a given meal, they have at least one. Other graduates find themselves making more frequent trips to the market to get what their bodies truly want. It is worth it because the quality of the eating experience is greatly enhanced and our bodies thrive on it.

Now look at your obstacles listed above and answer them by creating options based on Thin Within tools. You have more than enough information to create a 10 situation for every obstacle, and your family will love you for it! Kids deserve pleasers too!

You need never feel trapped by any situation again. Remember, you have options and you can plan. So whenever you feel like a victim, your freedom will come when you answer the following questions:

What are the obstacles here?

Why am I doing this?

What are my options?

What is the solution?

You are freeing your own genius by asking these questions. Trust yourself. Follow your answers.

THE WHERE-I-AM-TODAY QUESTIONNAIRE

Now comes the fun part. You are going to get to see how much progress you have made since you filled out the first Where-I've-Come-From Questionnaire. Fill out this questionnaire quickly, and be honest! Go back and compare the two questionnaires.

*Name*____
Age ____ *Height* ____ *Present Weight* ____ *Desired Weight* ____

On the following questions, circle the number that best applies:

6. How much of the time are you on a diet or sacrificing certain types of foods?

   1 2 3 4 5 6 7 8 9 10
   Always — Never

7. How frequently do you eat foods you really love?

   1 2 3 4 5 6 7 8 9 10
   Never — Always

8. How often do you think of yourself as a thin person?

   1 2 3 4 5 6 7 8 9 10
   Never — Always

9. Can you visualize or imagine yourself at your desired weight?

   1 2 3 4 5 6 7 8 9 10
   Never — Always

10. Do you think you are aware of your body's hunger and fullness signals?

    1 2 3 4 5 6 7 8 9 10
    Never — Always

Imagine that you had a fuel gauge for your stomach, much like that on a car, which registered how empty or full you were:

11. At what point on the gauge do you usually start eating?

0 1 2 3 4 5 6 7 8 9 10
Empty Comfy Stuffed

12. At what point on the gauge do you usually stop eating?

0 1 2 3 4 5 6 7 8 9 10
Empty Comfy Stuffed

What are your current concerns? *Rate each item listed below.*

13. Spending too much time worrying about your weight or eating behavior?

1 2 3 4 5 6 7 8 9 10
Serious Problem No Problem

14. Weighing frequently?

1 2 3 4 5 6 7 8 9 10
Serious Problem No Problem

15. Anorexia Nervosa?

1 2 3 4 5 6 7 8 9 10
Serious Problem No Problem

16. Bulimia?

1 2 3 4 5 6 7 8 9 10
Serious Problem No Problem

17. Disliking your body?

1 2 3 4 5 6 7 8 9 10
Serious Problem No Problem

18. Thinking too much about food?

1 2 3 4 5 6 7 8 9 10
Serious Problem No Problem

19. Snacking? (between meals or at night)

1 2 3 4 5 6 7 8 9 10
Serious Problem No Problem

20. Alcoholic beverages?

1 2 3 4 5 6 7 8 9 10
Serious Problem No Problem

21. Cigarettes?

1 2 3 4 5 6 7 8 9 10
Serious Problem No Problem

22. Feeling guilty about what you eat?

1 2 3 4 5 6 7 8 9 10
Serious Problem No Problem

23. Eating out of stress or boredom?

1 2 3 4 5 6 7 8 9 10
Serious Problem No Problem

24. Social eating? (parties, restaurants)

1 2 3 4 5 6 7 8 9 10
Serious Problem No Problem

In general, how do you rate your life in the following areas:

25. Health

1 2 3 4 5 6 7 8 9 10
Poor Excellent

26. Energy level

1 2 3 4 5 6 7 8 9 10
Low High

27. Physical activity

1 2 3 4 5 6 7 8 9 10
Sedentary Extremely Active

28. Productivity

1 2 3 4 5 6 7 8 9 10
Low High

29. Job satisfaction (consider student or housewife as a job)

1 2 3 4 5 6 7 8 9 10
Unsatisfying Very Satisfying

30. Close relationships (friends)

1 2 3 4 5 6 7 8 9 10
Unsatisfying Very Satisfying

31. Family relationships

1 2 3 4 5 6 7 8 9 10
Unsatisfying Very Satisfying

32. Sex life

1 2 3 4 5 6 7 8 9 10
Unsatisfying Very Satisfying

33. Ability to speak up for what you want

1 2 3 4 5 6 7 8 9 10
Difficult Easy

34. Level of self-esteem

1 2 3 4 5 6 7 8 9 10
Low High

SUCCESS TOOLS

• Whenever you feel stuck, reread this book. You'll feel realigned, you'll get back on purpose and move ahead with renewed enthusiasm.

• Continue saying Affirmations aloud and have a good time with it! The more you say it, the more you will believe it!

• Continue to fill in your Hunger Graph.

• Continue to mark your Observations and Corrections Chart.

• Use the Thin Within Keys to Weight Mastery.

THIN WITHIN SECRET

The irony of being fat:
We got fat eating diet *foods!*
The joy of Thin Within:
We stay thin
By eating the foods we love.

HUNGER GRAPH

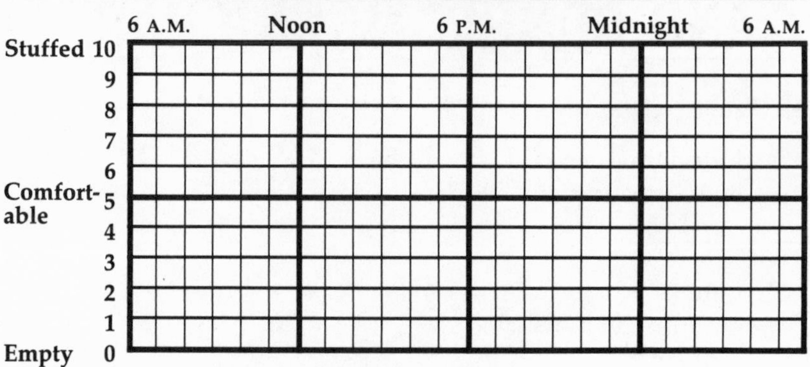

FOOD LOG

Enter all food and drink for 24 hours.	Time

THIN WITHIN OBSERVATIONS AND CORRECTIONS CHART

Observations	Day 29
1. I ate when my body was hungry.	
2. I ate in a calm environment by reducing distractions.	
3. I ate when I was sitting.	
4. I ate when my body and mind were relaxed.	
5. I ate and drank only the things my body *loved.*	
6. I paid attention only to my food while eating.	
7. I ate slowly, savoring each bite.	
8. I stopped before my body was full.	

DAY 30

The Flight of the Eagle

The secret of Thin Within is to turn every breakdown into a breakthrough, every problem into a possibility, and every loss into a win. This is done by creating permanent solutions at the level of the *cause* of a problem rather than looking for temporary solutions that don't work, or at best, only alleviate symptoms.

Diets rarely result in permanent weight loss because they don't address the *real* cause of a person's weight problem. A diet is a Band-Aid attempt to deal with excess pounds without looking in depth at what may be stimulating your Fat Machinery. Whatever the apparent cause is—upset feelings, boredom, fear, anger, stress, loneliness, sexuality, etc.—the *underlying belief* is "I don't deserve to be thin."

By using the tools in this book, the Thin Within Keys to Weight Mastery, Forgivenesses, Affirmations, Visualizations, and Daily Acknowledgments, you have changed that belief to "I *do* deserve to be thin." Once this is accomplished you are in present time and have mastery over your Fat Machinery.

Whenever you get stuck:

1. Ask yourself what belief is in the way of your total success.

2. Forgive yourself completely. (Write Forgivenesses 10 times.)

3. Create an appropriate affirmation (one that states a new belief, action, and result). Example: "I, ________________________, am naturally thin, eat 0 to 5, and I am a size 6."

4. As you write the affirmation be sure you allow your mind time to *share* its resistance. It is at that point that you'll hear the old, unworkable belief—"I can't wear a size 6! That's thinner than my mother."

5. Take that *resistance* and turn it into *assistance*:
"I, ________________________, am naturally thin, eat 0 to 5, and it is now safe for me to be thinner than my mother."

6. Then go back and complete your original affirmation (write it 10 times).

This process of changing ourselves at the level of substance through the use of Forgivenesses and Affirmations is the essence of Thin Within. It is why you *now* have weight mastery. It is also why the tools of Thin Within produce permanent results.

This is a book of freedom. These 30 days have been an introduction to the Thin Within life-style, which is one of 0 to 5 eating, deserving to have it all, and being filled with Forgivenesses and Affirmations. Understand that there is a delicate balance in this system, as if it were an ecosystem of the mind, body, and spirit. In order to have it all—you will want to maintain a balance and harmony in all three areas. You do this by using the Thin Within Keys to Weight Mastery and applying the Thin Within tools to change yourself at the level of belief.

Be patient with this process, knowing that, in Thin Within, patience is a kind of gentle anticipation. Like waiting for a flower to unfold, the process itself is enjoyable.

As this process lovingly occurs, remember you have been given the gift of discernment. This is the ability to choose on a moment-to-moment basis, knowing that you can trust the messages of your body.

After using the Thin Within tools for these 30 days, you have developed sensitive new antennae. You have become a discerning person who knows how to observe and correct yourself with compassion. This frees you to make creative, life-enhancing choices.

A NATURAL HARMONY

Thin Within's purpose has always been greater than merely to be a weight-loss program. It is to resolve issues with food, eating, and weight by creating a natural harmony among mind, body, and spirit.

In Thin Within we feel that less is more. If everyone ate 0 to 5, there would be enough food for those without. A life of quality, a life of pleasers, should be the heritage of everyone, not just a chosen few. By using the Thin Within Keys to Weight Mastery we will all be leaner, healthier, more energetic, and more creative.

This book may be ending, however, this is only the beginning of your Thin Within way of life. The more you use these tools and principles the more successful you will become.

You have been given all the keys to release yourself forever from that chicken coop. If you are ever tempted to go back to the safe, plump-chicken mentality, return instead to this book. It will remind you that you are free to fly. And throughout all the ups and downs of your life, always remember who you are: an eagle.

I have loved being with you for these 30 days. Go well, dear one. Be at peace and have fun. Allow yourself to discover who you truly are. Manifest on the outside the radiance you are on the inside. You are the gift that is wrapped by your body. You have mastery now, knowing exactly what to do to remain thin, satisfied, and filled with delight for the rest of your life. So take flight. The entire universe is your domain.

God bless you on your journey.

The Thin Within Way of Life

Now that you have completed the 30 days, how do you keep the inspiration and maintain the momentum?

First of all, gather people around you who understand your new Thin Within way of life. Thin Within represents a new-found freedom that is to be shared with family and friends, who also deserve to be set free from the tyranny of dieting. Dedicate one night per week to participating in a support group where you can share your experiences with those who have read or attended a Thin Within workshop. Setting goals, acknowledging your wins, and giving and receiving support are incredibly nuturing and will help you obtain those 10s in all areas of your life. To assist you in this process we have developed the Thin Within Support Group Packet, which explains how to organize a support group and contains invaluable information and suggestions to ensure your ongoing success.

Second, continue to use the tools that you have been given: the Hunger Graph, Food Log, Forgivenesses, Affirmations, Goal Setting, etc. The beauty of Thin Within is that it is now part of your life. It is not something you do on the side.

If you would like more information about Thin Within or the Support Group Packet please write to:

Thin Within
478 Santa Clara Ave. #300
Oakland, CA 94610

Index